PARLIAMENTARY DEMOCRACY IN UGANDA

The Experiment that Failed

Baganchwera N. I. Barungi

authorHOUSE®

AuthorHouse™
1663 Liberty Drive
Bloomington, IN 47403
www.authorhouse.com
Phone: 1-800-839-8640

First published by AuthorHouse   09/30/2011

ISBN: 978-1-4567-3592-0 (sc)
ISBN: 978-1-4567-3591-3 (hc)
ISBN: 978-1-4567-3590-6 (ebk)

Library of Congress Control Number: 2011901877

Printed in the United States of America

Any people depicted in stock imagery provided by Thinkstock are models,
and such images are being used for illustrative purposes only.
Certain stock imagery © Thinkstock.

This book is printed on acid-free paper.

This book is dedicated to my son, Bantu Barungi,
who passed on in 2007.

Foreword

Parliamentary Democracy in Uganda: the Experiment that Failed explores Uganda's malaise of armed dissidents, repression of political parties, military adventurism in neighbouring countries, grinding poverty in the countryside and political uncertainty arising from accumulated failure of successive regimes to cultivate a culture of peaceful transfer of power. In light of this, the democratisation process envisaged at the time of independence has been frustrated. The author sets out to unravel the cause of that frustration and impasse by tracing the beginning of Uganda's political institutions, particularly the central government organs established in the last century.

The new institutions and political organs were basically designed to forge Uganda ahead as a united and stable nation. An attempt is made to critically examine the foundations upon which these institutions were built. It is argued that the institutions were laid under a hostile environment of political diversity and multicultural heritage without an inbuilt balancing mechanism.

Accordingly the book recounts the difficult process of nation building undertaken in Uganda, with particular emphasis on the problems encountered in reconciling the new political institutions with the entrenched conservative traditional institutions in the South of the country. (The Buganda Agreement of 1900 and other agreements with the kingdoms of Ankole, Tooro and Bunyoro).

The author acknowledges the contribution made by the leaders of various political parties towards the task of nation building. It was a task undertaken amidst forces of feudalism and religious animosity. They were men and women of extraordinary foresight who had a clear vision of a new independent Uganda curved out of peoples of diverse cultural backgrounds. This book provides yet another vision of the future and suggests ideas how to overcome the political impasse that has bedevilled the country since independence.

Uganda has had two opportunities to put her political act together as a nation. The first missed opportunity was in 1967 when a new constitution was put in place. Conventional wisdom would have dictated seeking a fresh mandate from the electorate to endorse the radical changes incorporated in the new constitution. But political strategy and other considerations dictated otherwise. The end result was that the government of the day was confronted with problems of legitimacy. To many Ugandans the country appeared to be moving away from the agreed evolutionary process of democratisation towards militarism, which has totally engulfed Uganda's body politic.

The most recent missed opportunity occurred in 1994-95 when the process of making a new constitution was initiated. Unfortunately the exercise was flawed. In the first instance political party activities were banned. That meant party leaders and interest group leaders could not freely mobilise their members and supporters to solicit and articulate views of the electorate. The composition of the commission was not representative. In an effort to influence the outcome of the commission NRM (National Resistance Movement) secretariat prepared and distributed a prototype memorandum to local councils for submission to the commission. To confound matters the election of members to the Constituent Assembly (CA) was based on individual merit. Finally the Assembly was "packed" with nominated members whose function was to ensure that the aims and objectives of the NRM were entrenched in the constitution. Article 269 of the 1995 constitution was a product of that manipulation. Ideally membership of CA ought to have excluded sitting members of Parliament and those who intended to stand for the next parliament to ensure that members of the CA were not driven or motivated by narrow personal gains.

The 1995 Constitution stipulated a two-five year term limit. General Museveni's term of office was expected to end in 2006. That was not to be. The powers that be had different ideas. A vigorous campaign against the term limits was mounted and the ruling clique resorted to political intimidation and patronage, including monetary inducement to achieve that end. The incumbent Presidential Candidate secured a third term in an acrimonious general election that was characterised by unprecedented and massive rigging. But in the process a small window of hope was opened by repealing the notorious and obnoxious Article 269 of the Constitution, following great pressure exerted by political parties, religious institutions, and to some extent, the international community. The said article restricted political party activities to Party Headquarters in Kampala.

It is the hope of every well meaning Ugandan and well wishers in the international community that multiparty politics dispensation will last long enough to enable Ugandans build a peaceful, prosperous and democratic society with equal opportunities for all.

This is a book which fills a big gap in our recent political development.

Professor Edward J. B. Kakonge (Phd.)

Acknowledgements

I am grateful to my daughter Vernetta for spending her precious time typing the manuscript.

Special tribute goes to my wife, Adyeri Violet, and to my daughter, Atwoki Barbara, who were the prime source of inspiration in undertaking this project. I have been deeply touched by their constant encouragement, unfailing support and the coordinating role they have played throughout this work.

Opportunity is also taken to express my appreciation, through Barbara, to Elaine Carter and Ann Pattison of Johannesburg, South Africa who kindly assisted in typing the initial draft with all the unfamiliar Ugandan names of persons and places.

Many thanks are also due to Father Charles Ssengendo of the Kampala Archdiocese, in charge of the Archives Library, for allowing me free access to the Archdiocesan Library and to Sister Palma Bako Aziku of the Missionary Sisters of Mary Mother of the Church. To both of them I say, "Mwebale".

CONTENTS

Foreword		vii
Acknowledgements		xi
List of Abbreviations		xv
Chapter One	The Setting	1
Chapter Two	History Of Uganda	13
Chapter Three	Economic History Of Uganda	25
Chapter Four	Political Reforms Leading To Independence	33
Chapter Five	Uganda Attains Independence	43
Appendix 1	Letters Patent	49
Appendix 2	Members of Government of Uganda	51
Chapter Six	Evolution Of Political Institutions	57
Chapter Seven	The Lost Counties And The Constitutional Process	75
Chapter Eight	The Origin And Growth Of Uganda's Legislature	83
Chapter Nine	The Legislature At Work	97
Chapter Ten	Political Stability And Development	105
Chapter Eleven	Power Struggle And The Political Storm	113
Chapter Twelve	The Pigeonhole Constitution And The Ever Recurring Congo	127
Chapter Thirteen	The Common Man's Charter	147
Chapter Fourteen	The Rise Of Militarism In Uganda	157
Chapter Fifteen	Post-Amin Era	161
Chapter Sixteen	The Future	177
Chapter Seventeen	Conclusion	187
Bibliography		189

List of Abbreviations

ADF	Allied Defence Forces
CP	Conservative Party
DP	Democratic Party
HSA	Holy Spirit Army
IMF	International Monetary Fund
KY	Kabaka Yekka
LEGCO	Legislative Council
NCC	National Consultative Council
NRA	National Resistance Army
NRC	National Resistance Council
NRM	National Resistance Movement
RC	Resistance Council
UFM	Uganda Freedom Movement
UNO	Uganda Nationalist Organisation
UNLA	Uganda National Liberation Army
UNLF	Uganda National Liberation Front
UPA	Uganda People's Army
UPC	Uganda People's Congress
UPM	Uganda Patriotic Movement
UPU	Uganda People's Union
UNLA	Uganda Liberation Army
UNLF	Uganda Liberation Front
UNRF	Uganda Rescue Front
UPC	Uganda People's Congress

Chapter One

The Setting

Astride the equator on the plateau of east central Africa lies Uganda rimmed by high mountains and lakes. On the western border is the Great Rift Valley, containing Lakes Albert, Edward (Mwitanzige), and George (Rweru). In the south stretches Lake Victoria (Nalubale) the source of the river Nile (Kiyira). High mountains mark the north and eastern borders. From time immemorial the mighty River Nile and the high mountains in the west - the Mountains of the Moon (Rwenjura) have attracted attention from far and wide. The white man from a far-off land came to know the existence of the Nile and the fable Mountains. With the improvement in the means of transport and technological advancement, the white man set out to discover the mysteries of the source of the Nile and the legendary mountains. In the process the likes of John Hanning Speke, Richard Burton, James Grant and Henry Morton Stanley came face to face with the inhabitants of the land astride the equator. By coincidence the protracted explorations took place in the aftermath of the industrial revolution in Europe and in North America. Agricultural implements were improved. Industrialisation transforms agricultural economy into a commercial economy. This eases the demand on human labour to maintain large agricultural plantations of sugar, cotton and tobacco. In the 'New World' across the Atlantic, Africa happened to be the main source of the human labour provided by slaves forcibly transported to the New World. Partly to atone for the crimes committed against humanity by the slave traders, some righteous white men commonly known as philanthropists formed

1

associations and lobbies and began to campaign for the end of slave trade in Africa. The gentlemen of the cloth joined the philanthropists in the anti-slavery crusade. The campaign intensified following the declaration of the abolition of slavery. The Arabs did not seem to heed the declaration. The clash between the Arab slave traders and the white colonialists became inevitable. The colonial possessions in the New World had cast off the chains of colonialism and were now of age. They had control of their own destiny. Raw materials for industrial Europe became scarce. The European continental powers, including Britain, were compelled to look for new sources of raw materials. They turned to the 'Dark Continent'. The search for cheap new materials was characterised by rivalry among the great powers. To put an end to the rivalry, a conference was convened- the Berlin conference of 1884 which signaled the scramble and the partitioning of Africa. The continent was parcelled into spheres of influence, without any regard for ethnic or geographical boundaries. The land astride the equator, surrounded by Great Lakes and the legendary mountains fell under the British sphere of influence. The inhabitants of that land were lumped together for administrative purposes, despite the great diversity that existed in their cultural backgrounds. In the new set-up, Buganda occupied the central part neighbouring Bunyoro Kitara in the north-west. The two kingdoms boasted of centralised governments with their kings exercising immense political power. The invaders acknowledged this fact but continued to subdue the kingdoms. In the south-west lies Ankole (Karokarungi) with a multiplicity of principalities. These were merged under British tutelage. The same was done in Busoga where a multiplicity of even smaller principalities existed. In the extreme south-west and at the foothills of Mount Elgon one comes across the Bakiga and the Bagisu without any recognised institution of chieftainship or an institutionalised political authority. Here, the biggest cultural organisation was the clan.

The Bagisu were organised on the basis of patrilineages. The lineages are not only of descent groups but also territorial units varying in size. It is the individual units based on the minor lineage that provides political leadership and authority. The Mugasya wields authority as a war leader, arbitrator and guide. A council of elders elects him - an element of democracy. What is interesting here is that there is complete separation between temporal authority and spiritual authority. Land is jealously guarded. In the north, Acholi and Langi offer examples of more open societies with their social and political structures based on clans but organised well enough to ensure the security of the entire communities through dialogue by the council of elders. There are powerful chiefs - the Rwots, with considerable political authority. But the new masters refuse to recognise them as hereditary rulers and accord them appropriate status. This is partly because by the time the north was brought under the protectorate, the sphere of influence had already been defined. The rush for concluding treaties with the native chiefs had long passed. In the west of the Nile we learn from oral history that Sudanic groups first crossed from the Albert Nile about fourteen generations ago. The inhabitants consist of Alur, Madhi, Okebo and Lendu. They are divided into patrilineal clans with a series of eponymous-segmented divisions. The sections of clans come under the authority of recognised hereditary heads. Within the clans the direct descendants of the groups who crossed the Albert Nile are regarded as noble. They have settled and acquired positions of authority. The Atyak clan comes to mind. Unlike the Bagisu, the noble chiefs combine both temporal and spiritual powers. They enjoy supernatural powers and claim to communicate with the community's ancestors. Their authority is not centralised. They have no organisation to exert coercive power. Their primary function is to settle disputes between warring clan sections. In effect, the clans form segmented states as opposed to the acephalous-segmented societies and the multiple kingdoms of the south based on nationalities. But the hereditary element subsists to the lowest level.

This was the state of the different political and social structures that obtained when the British proclaimed a protectorate over present-day Uganda. Most of the political and social structures were retained with a few modifications. The notion of a nation-state was non-existent. The chiefs across the country became 'Nyampara' (headmen). British hegemony was established but not without a fight. Kings, chiefs and clan leaders in their respective areas put up some resistance. The stiffest resistance happens to be that offered by Kabaka Mwanga of Buganda and Kabalega of Bunyoro Kitara. The threat of annexation came from two fronts. From the north the threat was perpetrated by Muhammad Ali, an Albanian national acting in the name of the Sultan of Turkey who had established his family as the ruling dynasty of Egypt. He extended his authority up the Nile as far as Gondokoro. He wanted to extend his jurisdiction to the Great Lakes region. To achieve his objective, he enlisted the services of European officials. The rampant slave trade going on in the region hampered the work of the European officials. Their energies were diverted to stamping out the Arab slave trade. Little was achieved in this regard. In the meantime, Egypt proclaimed jurisdiction over Equatorial province.

Sir Samuel Baker made a bid to annex Bunyoro Kitara as part of a new Egyptian province. Baker was essentially an explorer and his ambition was to discover the source of the Nile. But Speke managed to snatch that opportunity from him. To compensate for the loss of the prestige the discovery of the source of the Nile would have bestowed upon him, he turned his energies to extending Egyptian rule over the whole basin of the Nile. It so happens that at the time the great colonial powers, Germany, France, Britain, Portugal, Belgium and the Netherlands which were to congregate at the Berlin Conference to partition the continent were indifferent to territorial acquisition. Baker took advantage of the situation and established defence posts in present-day Acholi. The garrisons were manned by Egyptian and Sudanese soldiers. Imbued with extraordinary personal ambition, he sought to impose his authority further south. There he met his match in the person of Kabalega, Kamurasi's successor. The late Omukama Kamurasi had earlier on played host to Baker and his wife along with Speke and Grant. Kabalega was fully aware of Baker's designs. He was therefore constrained to extend to him the courtesies he had earlier enjoyed during his three month stay at the royal court. Despite the Omukama's protest, Baker proclaimed the kingdom of Bunyoro Kitara part of the Egyptian Empire. In response Omukama Kabalega declared war on the invader. The latter was militarily overwhelmed and manageed to escape across the Nile in a great hurry. Kabalega's timely action coupled with the Sudan Revolt led by Muhammad Ahmed, "The Madhi" ended the adventures of Baker and his principals. Baker turned his humiliation into hatred. Kabalega's perceived bad image by the subsequent British colonial administrators and sundry emanated from Baker's writings after his defeat by the African king. Revenge was the next thing. Internally, Baker's exit and the removal of the northern threat brought about a change of heart on the part of Kabaka Mutesa I. Stanley had urged Mutesa to request Christian missionaries to come to Buganda and teach his people. On their arrival he discovered that they were not in position to provide him with the military protection he longed for. His attitude towards them dramatically changed. The underlying reason for the change is simple. The impending threat of annexation from Egypt was no more. However, he still had to contend with Buganda's age-long rival, Bunyoro Kitara whose decline Kabalega had brought to an end. Buganda saw no alternative but to embrace the British invaders for reasons that would in modern times be called state security. Mutesa's instinct of self-preservation must have been extraordinary. His successor Kabaka Mwanga, often portrayed as a villain, appears to have had a better perception of what the whites were about. Mwanga's efforts to preserve the territorial integrity and independence of his kingdom came to naught. There were internal contradictions that had been introduced in the Buganda society by the agents of colonialism viz. the senior chiefs and other ranks. The newly converted Christians split into two factions, the Protestants and Catholics. To these factions add the Muslims and, of course, the traditionalists whose loyalty to the throne was unshakeable. Division and factionalism within the kingdom became the order of the day. To be sure, a house divided against itself cannot triumph. What is worse, power shifted from the throne to the landed gentry who happen to be the chiefs at all levels. They were also part and parcel of the colonial administrative machinery and were completely divorced from the wishes and aspirations of the population.

These are the men, together with their counterparts in the rest of Uganda, whom a certain historian described nearer to the time of independence as older women and men who had exercised authority under the colonial regime and who looked towards a future controlled by African political leaders with some trepidation.

The take-over by African politicians from the entrenched colonialists is not plain sailing, as most people would like us to believe. It takes decades before a concerted resurgence of nationalism emerges. The events of the Second World War provided a conducive environment for the oppressed people in the colonies to demand the right to self-determination. Britain let go the Indian sub-continent. Radical nationalism gripped the British colonial possessions in West Africa. Ghana or rather Gold Coast, under Kwame Nkrumah, spearheaded the campaign for freedom. Ugandans did not remain indifferent to these developments. They started in a small way at a non-national level.

Groups of political agitators demanded the democratisation of the Buganda Lukiko. The land tenure system introduced under the 1900 Agreement became a bone of contention. The non-participation of the indigenous people in the spinning of cotton and the processing of coffee was questioned by the very peasants who produced the two crops. Other farmers joined the growers in Buganda throughout the country. The people of Uganda started identifying their common interests. They argued that the only plausible remedy to economic exploitation was the attainment of political freedom at the national level, which meant self-government.

The riots of 1945 and 1949 in Buganda had a great impact on the central government. To contain the situation, the government had to rely more on coercive power otherwise known in ordinary language as force, be it the military or the police. Force proved inadequate for purposes of political stability and economic progress. The need for change became inevitable. The government embarked on the process of democratisation or rather decolonisation. The legislative council until then an exclusive club for white businessmen and Asian traders opened its doors to the Africans. To hoodwink the radical nationalists, the four seats allotted to the Africans were filled by members of the colonial establishment, the topmost chiefs one from each province, namely the Katikiros and the secretary-generals. They passed as representatives of Buganda, western kingdoms, and the eastern and northern provinces. Meanwhile, new laws were promulgated to regulate the activities of the trade unions and farmers' associations. Government-controlled co-operative societies were established and debarred from affiliating to political organisations. This crippled the national movement for self-government. By early 1950s political parties began to appear on the scene e.g. the Uganda National Congress (UNC), the Democratic Party (DP) and many others. The tide for self-government could not be halted. Further changes took place in the legislative council. The number of African representatives was increased to fourteen. The district councils acting as electoral colleges elected eleven representatives. The Buganda Lukikio nominated three. The switch to district representation in the legislative council rather than provincial representation created new problems. It enhanced the feeling of tribalism, as the colonialists were wont to say. The changes rekindled old fears within the circles of Mengo establishment. They argued that development and strengthening of the legislative council as a national institution was likely to eclipse the Lukiko and to reduce the status of Buganda within the framework of Uganda.

In June 30, 1953 the Secretary of State made a casual after-dinner remark about closer East African union. The remarks sent a wrong signal to the Mengo establishment. The ministers and the Lukiko members over-reacted. A political crisis ensued. The Kabaka was deeply involved. The kingdom of Buganda demanded independence and a timetable. Matters came to a head. Britain withdrew recognition from Mutesa II as Kabaka of Buganda. He was deported to Great Britain. Government work in the kingdom grinded to a halt. By tradition nothing moves without the Kabaka.

However, political analysts assert that the indignation and protest over the issue of closer union was a smoke-screen. The real reason was fear of the growing importance of Legislative Council (LEGCO) as a representative body for the whole country and a focal point for political activity. It is this, more than anything else, that was perceived as threatening Buganda's position.

This period marked the beginning of a renewed spirit of separatism in respect to Buganda. To rectify the situation and in an effort to bring Buganda back to the fold, Sir Kenneth Hancock, Director of the Institute of Commonwealth Studies, was invited to Uganda in 1954. He held discussions with the Mengo establishment leadership in search of a settlement. They struck a compromise. At the same time the colonial administration worked out constitutional reforms for the whole country to transform LEGCO into a national forum. A ministerial system of government was introduced with five ministers, three of whom were Africans. The council membership shot up to sixty. Africans filled up thirty of the sixty seats. As part of the Hancock bargain, Buganda made a solemn undertaking to participate in the future reformed LEGCO.

Within the scope of the new political framework the Kabaka was insulated from the vagaries of politics by instituting a constitutional monarchy. The device did not work because Kiganda traditions do not permit the exclusion of the Kabaka from active administration of his kingdom.

The Ministers were either not radical enough or lacked the courage to take full advantage of the constitutional innovation that excluded the Kabaka from active politics. With hindsight, if that provision had been implemented, perhaps Mutesa's impulse to become president of Uganda in the early 1960s would have been dampened. The political crisis of 1966 might have been averted. The events of 1964-1966 could have taken a different course, without the Kabaka being involved.

Back to the significance of 1955 reforms: the reforms aimed at drawing Buganda into the main stream of national politics and to bring home to the Mengo establishment that Buganda's destiny was entwined with Uganda's destiny - the two had a common destiny. Realism demanded of the Buganda ultra- traditionalists to regard Buganda as an integral part of independent Uganda. The reforms were accepted by all parties, politicians and the business community. For the next three years harmony prevailed between the central government and Buganda. Relations between Buganda and the rest of the country were at their best. It was the way forward. Progress in the economic field was commendable. For all intents and purposes, Uganda was poised to move forward as a united prosperous country with all her rich diverse cultural background. The outlook all around was good.

The emergence of political parties brought about a new dimension. Several political parties came into being as if to reflect and to emphasise the pluralistic nature of the Ugandan society. In the end only two national parties survived the harassment by the colonial administration and intimidation by the traditionalists. The survivors were the Uganda Peoples Congress, an offshoot of the Uganda National Congress and the Democratic Party. The two spearheaded in earnest the campaign for self-government. The parties cut across ethnic boundaries. But both retained religious affiliation. The drama of religious animosity experienced in the 1880s and early 1890s in Buganda repeated itself, initially in the same area but spread to other parts of the country under the auspices of the Democratic Party. On the other hand, the Protestant establishment could not let go its ascendancy in political affairs it had enjoyed ever since the religious wars of 1894. The Catholics were adamant and determined to turn the tables and to end the political marginalisation to which they had been subjected for so long. In the circumstances the task of building viable political institutions was not on the agenda. Both parties turned to makeshift social political forces. The Kabaka Yekka was such a force brought into being to curtail the activities of the Democratic Party in Buganda and, indeed, to ensure its defeat in the 1962 polls.

Much as each political party tried in public to distance itself from religious orientation, behind the scenes the picture was different. It is possible that there was no escape from that scenario, given the pattern of education in those days. During the colonial period competing Christian missionaries founded most of the leading schools. Religious animosity and prejudice were almost part of the schools curricula.

In the absence of a well-defined political ideology by the political parties, the use of religion as a front became attractive because it provided a ready audience among the ordinary Ugandans. In the final analysis the Uganda Peoples Congress was believed to symbolise the Protestant church and its adherents, while the Democratic Party masqueraded as a liberator of Catholics from Protestant chauvinism. Granted that this was divisive politics, but it was no excuse for current leaders of government to ban the institution of political parties per se. The blame must be apportioned to the leadership of such organisations. The root of the problem is the way foreign religions were introduced in the country. So, any blanket condemnation of political parties as a source of instability was simply misplaced and was simplistic in form and content.

In 1958 direct elections were introduced in the Legislative Council. But the real test for the African leaders came the following year. The appointment of the Wild Committee made it possible for the population at large, irrespective of race or religion, to express views on the future Uganda they would like to see. The terms of reference for the committee sent different signals to different groups. To the leaders of political parties the signal was clear: Britain that once boasted that the sun never sets on the British Empire was now in retreat. The question was who was to fill the void created by the British exit? The task was to capture power and the race started immediately. In the process splits within the parties occurred. Mergers and realignment followed the splits. Political activity was at its highest.

The protracted constitutional reforms sent shivers to the ultra-traditionalists. But they quickly composed themselves in the false belief that the retreating colonial power would simply hand over to the hereditary rulers with whom hurriedly prepared agreements had been signed at the beginning of colonial rule. On that assumption the British would simply terminate the agreements and political authority would revert to the hereditary rulers and paramount chiefs right across the country with perhaps some modification to suit the changed conditions.

This became a bone of contention between the nationalists and the traditionalists. It was the genesis of discord that was to destabilise independent Uganda to the point of complete breakdown of law and order. Nonetheless, independence was achieved. The first three years of independence turned out to be Uganda's political golden age. Everything seemed to be going according to plan and under control. Parliament was in place representing every social spectrum of society. There were African, Asian and European representatives. Members of Parliament were responsible to the electorate. The cabinet composed of capable men was going about its work with speed and efficiency. It was sufficiently transparent and accountable to parliament. The public service was functioning well and full of prospects for greater advancement. Security of tenure was guaranteed. Corruption was regarded as an abominable crime. To cap it all, a new office of ceremonial president was established with well-defined functions to perform. The Kabaka of Buganda occupied the high office. There was enough peace to stimulate meaningful economic advancement and to provide gainful employment to the majority of the population.

Medicare, education and other social services were within reach of every citizen. Above all, there was respect for authority and the rule of law was the bedrock for governance.

In the realm of foreign affairs the country was at peace with its immediate neighbours. Its image abroad was as good as it could be. The security forces were well-disciplined and were subjected to civilian authority.

Signs of trouble started appearing on the horizon in 1964 as exemplified by the collapse of the KY-UPC alliance, the referendum in the lost counties, the shabby ousting of the secretary general of the ruling party at the Gulu delegates' conference and the Congolese gold affair blown out of proportion by Daudi Ochieng. Then came the abrogation of the 1962 Constitution and the detention of five cabinet ministers. Dan M. Mudola states: "With the promulgation of the 1962 Independence Constitution, the historic interest groups, namely, the religious and ethnic groups had triumphed. The constitutional formula basically served the interests of these groups and would only be adhered to the extent that their interests would be served." *Religion, Ethnicity and Politics in Uganda* (1993 p. 25). The holding of the referendum in the lost counties claimed by Bunyoro was not in the interests of Buganda. (See chapter on Lost Counties.) The alliance between the Uganda Peoples Congress and the Kabaka Yekka could no longer be justified and sustained. It collapsed and set in motion a chain reaction of events culminating in the 1966 crisis.

The post-1966 'revolution' period changed the pattern of politics in Uganda. The Security Forces, particularly the Army and the General Service Intelligence unit, came into prominence. Earlier on in 1964 a mutiny took place in Jinja. With the help of British troops the mutiny was suppressed. But no steps were taken to reorganise the army on a sound basis and to turn it into a national institution. Its composition remained lopsided in favour of the North. In the aftermath of the mutiny the need for a multi-ethnic army was raised in parliament. Felix Onama, Minister of Defence, did not entertain such a proposal. On the contrary, he proceeded to purge the army of most commissioned southern officers after the crisis of 1966. The effect was that the population from the south felt alienated from the army. The idea that the south could never gain power without a military establishment of their own began to gain currency. The security measures taken by the government after the abrogation of 1962 left a lot to be desired. A state of emergency was declared in Buganda, renewable at intervals of six months. A large number of prominent opposition leaders, including the Democratic Party chief, were detained. General apathy hit the country. Parliament hitherto known for its critical stance of unpalatable government policies became compliant. Political party district chiefs of the Uganda Peoples Congress were defiant. The party machinery at the lower levels broke down. The annual delegates' conference took place in 1968 but internal democratic process within the party hierarchy had been abandoned. After the 'Lugogo fire', that is an attempt on the life of Milton Obote, the idea of a one-party state was contemplated by some members of the ruling party. Government refused to implement the recommendation.

The effect of the announcement concerning a one-party state made after the Annual Delegates Conference was that all political avenues for an alternative government were presumed closed. The only option open to the other political groups, which did not share the views of the ruling party, was subversion. These comprised of the Democratic Party, which during the golden years of parliamentary democracy was the Official Opposition. Buganda whose many leaders were either in detention or in exile and to some extent the western kingdoms and other ethnic groups felt marginalised. A republican constitution was in force. In this instance, Parliament acted as a constituent assembly by debating and passing the Republican Constitution. The leadership failed to send members of parliament to the country to seek a fresh mandate and thereby secure a popular endorsement of the new constitution. The legitimacy of the constitution remained in question. Demagogues in future used that flaw to condemn and disown it. Having overcome the political storm, Milton Obote turned his attention to a new political ideology, an ideology that could pass as homegrown. A Common Man's Charter was published in October 1969. A new political philosophy supposedly Uganda's own product, 'The Move to the Left' was launched. To a close observer the move to the left turned out to be socialistic-oriented. It spelt doom for the capitalist interests of the Western Powers in the region. It would have exposed and isolated Kenyatta's Kenya since Tanzania was in the process of building a socialistic pattern of society. In the context of the politics of the cold war the move to the left by Uganda could not be tolerated.

The government of the day had to go. The American-led capitalists had the capacity to remove the author of the charter and his government from power. The army became a convenient tool for the job. In 1963 Uganda and Israel started developing diplomatic relations. By the mid-1960s the two countries were exchanging high-powered delegations. Consequently,

Israel personnel began training military police and intelligence manpower for Uganda. They accomplished this task with Jewish thoroughness. At the same time, they used their presence in Uganda to ferry arms to Sudan for Sudanese dissidents. The Ugandan government upon discovering their nefarious activities threatened Israel mission with expulsion. In the circumstances Israel, acting on behalf of the Western Powers, was only too eager to use its contact within the security forces to topple the Ugandan government through their crony, Idi Amin. They were in such a pivotal position that they were able to choose and pick the person who would lead the coup d'etat. Among the candidates for the job was Defence Minister, Felix Onama, who was brushed aside at the last minute. Amin was considered to be more pliant and, therefore, likely to promote and safeguard the interests of the West.

To prepare the political ground for the coup and to arouse popular discontent, the government was hit by shortage of foreign exchange earnings deliberately caused by foreign monopolies taking more money out of the country than they were bringing in. Imported goods were in short supply. Producer prices fell. The ordinary people were hard pressed by the high cost of living. All these aroused popular discontent. Eventually, the army acting as a tool of imperialist interests and manipulation, overthrew the government.

Chapter Two

History Of Uganda

"The wretched missionaries are dragging us into the centre of Africa, our burden is too great, we have too much of the world".[1]

Writers before me have written volumes on the history of Uganda especially that part of her colonial history. This work is primarily a political analysis and will not devote much space to history. It will suffice to remind readers that Uganda like many other Third World countries fell prey to colonialism. It was one of the British dependencies in East Africa administered solely for British colonial interests. However, the annexation of the various 'Native Kingdoms and Chieftainships' which make up today's Uganda presents an interesting study for a student of imperialism. Britain and her imperialist agents employed various methods to accomplish the annexation. In the words of Ken Saro Wiwa of Nigeria: "In 1884 European powers gathered in Berlin to carve up the African continent along water courses and lines of longitude and latitude on a map" He goes on to say: "Old African empires were destroyed in the new structures which resulted from the misadventure, and several cultures were henceforth forced to live under the same roof…" He concludes: "The pacification exercise meant the destruction of peoples, of ways of life, and it took different forms in different regions of Black Africa".[2]

1   William Ewart Gladstone, British Prime Minister (1868-74; 1880-85; 1886; 1892-3):

2   *A month and a Day, A Detention Diary* (Penguin Books) p183-4

In Uganda the forms of destruction adopted by the British were persuasion by way of agreements and disorientation through foreign religious teachings, each of which was sanctioned by sheer force of arms – the maxim gun was the supreme weapon.

European contact with Uganda took place during the reigns of Kabaka Mutesa I of Buganda and Omukama Kamurasi of Bunyoro Kitara. They ruled between 1852 and 1884. The two kings witnessed the beginning of the colonial era but did not suffer the brunt of humiliation and indignity inflicted on their successors, namely, Kabaka Mwanga and Omukama Kabalega Chwa II Rumoma Mahanga. The two successors had to grapple with the onset of colonialism, which eventually destroyed their kingdoms. Let me start with Buganda. The primary task of the early British colonial administrators was to subdue Buganda and Bunyoro. Lord Lugard then Captain in the service of the Imperial British East African Company played a decisive role in the annexation operation.

Professor Kenneth Ingham describes Kabaka Mwanga as "a young man of weak character unable to dominate the situation in which he found himself save for brief periods and by ill considered acts of violence".[3] While not condoning the violence meted out to the young Christians, the professor's assertion is an unfair judgement considering the various destabilising forces that were directed against the person of the Kabaka and his kingdom. First, the number of Arab traders had substantially increased. These traders had converted many indigenous people to Islam. Secondly, following his predecessor's induced invitation to European missionaries, the mission of evangelisation had been stepped up. A lot of his subjects were converted to the new religion of Christianity. The Christians were divided into Catholics and Protestants. There was a third group of African traditionalists who identified themselves with the Kabaka and the African way of life. The Arabs and their followers were suspicious of the activities of the Christian missionaries and did everything they could to instill fear in the mind of the King that the missionaries were out to undermine his authority.

The situation became exacerbated when Bishop Hannington was murdered allegedly on the instructions of the Kabaka. We now know that the allegation was unfounded. Be that as it may, the missionaries got extremely scared. They could not trust Kabaka Mwanga for their protection. They wanted another authority less "arbitrary and murderous". Of course, that could only mean European authority. At the same time,

3   *History of East Africa* (Longmans 1962) p145.

the young and ambitious Baganda converts felt equally insecure. The stage was set for a rebellion against the Kabaka.

In 1888 the young Christians ganged up with the Moslems and forced Mwanga off the throne. The brief reconciliation between the Christians and the Moslems brought Kiwewa, brother to Mwanga, to power. But the reconciliation was short-lived. The Moslem adherents evicted the Christians. The Christians together with the missionaries fled to Ankole. Almost a year later the Christians in exile worked out a rapprochement with Mwanga and with the help of Charlie Stokes, previously a missionary now turned arms trader, intercepted a supply of arms and ammunition meant for the Moslems and succeeded in fighting their way back to the control of the country. By then Buganda was firmly under the influence of the missionaries through their association with the converts who had banded themselves together into a new Baganda organism of the Christian party. The real showdown for Mwanga was yet to come. Having got rid of the Moslems, a feud for power began within the ranks of the Christians – the Protestants and the Catholics. War broke out between the two contending groups in 1892. The rival Christians were headed by "Mackay, the earnest uncompromising Calvinist, and Lourdel, the equally tenacious son of rural France".[4] Captain Lugard who was under instructions to pacify Uganda (read Buganda) was obliged to intervene to ensure that British power emerged supreme. One must also add that the captain had strong ties with the Church Missionary Society. Lugard's maxim gun tipped the balance. The battle of Mengo marked the end of the sovereignty of Buganda when she was forced to fly the British flag, which hitherto Mwanga had refused to do. Before the showdown, Mwanga had given an undertaking to allow complete religious freedom. The spoils of office were divided among the Protestants and Catholics. A religious divisive element was thus planted in the body politic of future Uganda. A Protestant adherent was installed as Katikiro of Buganda. He was Apollo Kagwa about whom I shall comment later. After the restoration of Mwanga to the throne and the enhanced Christian hegemony, *The Times of London*, (1888), quoting the old saying, wrote as follows:

"The blood of martyrs is the seed of the church. On the success of the Uganda experiment, with its alternation of favourable and adverse circumstances, depends the happiness of the interior of the vast continent for generations." That was the volatile and confused state of affairs in Buganda

4   Thomas and Scott, *Uganda* (Oxford University Press London: Humphrey Milford 1935) p24.

when the Heligoland Treaty came into effect that settled colonial rivalry between Germany and Britain over central and East African possessions. It was in the light of that treaty that Captain Lugard was dispatched to Uganda to take effective control of the territory. He accordingly made full use of his maxim gun to force a settlement on the warring factions that were up in arms against the Kabaka. From then on, Lugard continuously intervened in local disputes among the Baganda chiefs. Back to the battle of Mengo: chieftainships were redistributed among the victorious Protestant and the vanquished Catholics and Moslems. Both the Catholics and Moslems felt they had been marginalised. In the end it was Mwanga who was the greatest loser, as Thomas and Scott put it: "Mwanga, largely shorn of the veneration of his subjects, no longer commanded unquestioned compliance with his decisions. He was obliged to subordinate his authority to that of the British Sub-Commissioner in charge of Buganda": *Uganda* (p.29). The Kabaka was once fined for "illegal trafficking in ivory". To make things worse, Mwanga's royal assembly, 'the Lukiko', ceased to meet under his own presidency but under that of a British officer".[5] It is understandable that most Baganda traditionalists, often referred to as 'pagans' by the colonial historians, found it difficult to accommodate themselves to the new British conditions to which the Kabaka had been subjected. The obvious followed - restlessness from 1893 to 1897 when the Kabaka escaped from his capital and staged a rebellion against the British administration. His people as expected rallied around him. Unfortunately, his chiefs were divided. Their loyalty was suspect. Strange as it may seem, their loyalty was more to the British administration and the missionaries than to their Kabaka and their country. Professor Kenneth Ingham says: "Many of the chiefs held the British in great respect for the knowledge they had brought to Uganda (read Buganda); others recognised that their own positions and status had been largely achieved through their adherence to the white invaders".[6] With that lot as chiefs, Kabaka Mwanga was summarily deposed. David Chwa was proclaimed the new Kabaka. He was only four years old. But Mwanga's overthrow was not without a fight. It may be recalled that after Captain Lugard had secured Mwanga's signature to the 'treaty', he moved fast to pacify Buganda and the rest of Uganda as instructed. He thus conceived the idea of enlisting Sudanese troops who had remained in Equatoria, following the departure of Stanley and Emin Pasha in 1889 and who had settled near the South end of Lake

5   *Report by Ternan to Salisbury January 25, 1897, F.O. 2/132.*
6   *History of East Africa* (Longmans 1962) p183.

Albert (Mwitanzige). The Captain went over, and got about 8000 troops. On his way back he stationed some of them along the newly constructed line of forts on the southern border of Bunyoro. The rest he brought with him to Entebbe (then known as Port Alice). It was those troops at Entebbe he used to settle the war between the Catholics and the Protestants. The same troops were used to fight Mwanga and his loyal chiefs who staged an outstanding resistance in Masaka against the foreign invaders. Mwanga and his men were outclassed but he managed to work his way to the North of Bunyoro where he joined Kabalega.

Omukama Kabalega had once again taken centre stage as a rallying point for the Sudanese mutineers. Had it not been for the fresh reinforcement of Indian troops the Kabalega – Mwanga episode could easily have been different. The war had then taken on a racial turn. It was the Africans against white invaders. The indigenous people of Uganda (Banyoro, Baganda, Langi) and the Sudanese soldiers had joined hands to fight agents of white imperialism. Because Kabaka Mwanga had been vilified by a host of writers on unspecified grounds it is incumbent upon the young generation, detached from old prejudices, to have a fresh look at the history of our political development by focussing on the role played by men like Mwanga who by accident of history found themselves on the wrong side of the colonial masters.

I have no doubt that the Kabaka, by the very nature of his background and the environment in which he was brought up, was in order to accept no command from anybody. He also had a moral obligation as a custodian of customs and traditions of his people to tread cautiously in respect of a new and foreign mode of life. As a king, his first preoccupation must have been to maintain his authority and preserve Kiganda customs and traditions as modified from time to time. The wholesale condemnation of African culture by the white missionaries was motivated, not by spiritual considerations, but rather by arrogance bordering on white superiority complex. Let us be objective by accepting the fact that man is not wholly virtuous and in the same vein we must realise that he is not wholly vicious either.

It is in this context that one ought to analyse what became of the Kingdom of Buganda after the fall of Mwanga. The Kabaka's reaction to foreign rule was a reflection of what many of his subjects felt. Thomas and Scott explain: "In July 1897, it became known that certain chiefs in Buganda were planning to revolt. King Mwanga, chafing under the checks which an ordered government was imposing upon him, was doubtless privy to a design which seemed to offer him freedom, but he lost his nerve and fled to Buddu where a large gathering of disaffected gathered around him".[7] Thereafter, a minor was crowned king. Regents were appointed to run the affairs of Buganda. Apollo Kagwa was the most dominant of the three regents. From then on we can say, without fear of contradiction, the power base shifted from the throne to the Katikiro who, together with the chiefs wielded immense power. But I am compelled to add that real power behind Apollo Kagwa and the chiefs was the British Assistant Commissioner in Buganda.

Having dealt a fatal blow to the old system in Buganda through intrigue and civil strife, the colonial administration proceeded to consolidate their hold on their new possession in Africa's heartland. The next target was Bunyoro Kitara, which throughout the period of civil war in Buganda, gave refuge to the groups opposed to the foreign invaders. In the case of Kabaka Kalema, military assistance was extended to him and his men. Thomas and Scott clearly state: "Because Bunyoro offered a harborage for disaffected elements, it constituted a continual threat to peace and Macdonald now planned its conquest with the assistance of Buganda army". They continue: "The plan conformed conveniently with instructions which had been received to counter a suspected forward movement of the Belgians towards the Albert Nile".[8] Let me at the outset point out that political power of Bunyoro-Kitara at that time extended far afield than any other existing kingdom in the region. According to the elders of Bunyoro, the power of Bunyoro – Kitara stretched from the Nile in the East to beyond River Semiliki in the West and from the Nile in the north to Buhweju Hills in the south. Runyoro language was well understood in the region. In addition, the kingdom exercised great diplomatic influence in the surrounding areas, particularly in Busoga, West Nile, Acholi, Lango and parts of Teso. In contrast to its present-day standing and what is left of it, The Bunyoro-Kitara of the 18th century enjoyed a healthy and vibrant economy. It maintained the greatest stock of foodstuffs in the region. It had enormous resources of salt, iron deposits and ivory, let alone its military might. By the time of the British invasion in 1893 the kingdom's regular army numbered about 20,000 men, equipped with guns and rifles. Because of its economic strength described above, it was able to maintain a large

---

7   *Uganda* (Oxford University Press, London: Humphrey Milford 1935) pp 36, 37.

8   *Uganda* (Oxford University Press, London: Humphrey Milford 1935) p.35.

army. Let us now turn to the man who bore the biggest brunt of colonial oppression, Omukama Kabalega Chwa II Rumoma Mahanga.

Kabalega succeeded his father, Kamurasi, in the year 1871. His accession to the throne was preceded by a civil war. Kabalega had three contenders to the throne to deal with. He emerged victorious. He then set out to build his army so as to be able to consolidate his position, to regain Bunyoro-Kitara's lost territories and to restore the Kingdom's greatness and glory. The authority of the King had greatly been weakened during Kamurasi's reign. A number of princes had rebelled and seceded. Prince Kaboyo in Toro and Prince Ruyonga in Chope had declared unilateral independence. By raising a standing army Kabalega departed from the traditional pattern of relying on the general public, not only for the safety and protection of the King, but also for the defence of the Kingdom. His was a novel and revolutionary idea in the lacustrine region of East Africa. The newly established army was divided into divisions or battalions known as 'bitongole'. Each 'kitongole' (singular) was headed by a Supreme Commander/General. The general was known as 'Engabwa y'Omukama'. The Commander was decorated with a string of beads, which he wore around his neck, signifying that he represented the Crown. The most outstanding generals of the Omukama Kabalega in the new army were Byabachwezi, Rwabudongo, Ireta Byangombe and Kikukule Runego. All of them, except Rwabudongo, doubled as chiefs.

Byabachwezi of Mumwoli clan succeeded his father, Nyakamatura Nyakatura, as saza chief. He was commander of the battalion known as Ekibale located right in the heart of Bunyoro Kitara, the present Bugahya county. He was the longest surviving general of Kabalega. He became Chief Minister or Katikiro under the British but was never reconciled with them. He played a significant part in the rebellion or rather the passive resistance of 1901 known as Ekyanyangire ostensibly directed against Baganda chiefs introduced in Bunyoro after the fall of Kabalega. He was indeed the rallying point for resistance and was punished heavily by the British administration for that. He was too influential to be dismissed for fear of another uprising. Byabachwezi died in 1912 and was succeeded by his son, Zakayo Jawe, as Saza Chief.

Rwabudongo was in charge of the Kihambya battalion and proved to be one of the greatest generals. He belonged to the Abahamba clan whose totem is a musogasoga tree. He was the treasurer of the army and held a position that in modern terminology would be termed quarter-master general. The late Akio Wamala Kamese, who is remembered for having laid the foundation for the Cooperative Movement in Bunyoro and initiator of various developmental cooperative projects in the kingdom, was Rwabudongo's grandson.

General Kikukule Runega also combined the offices of Saza Chief and Commander of the 'Ekibanja' battalion that was charged with the task of defending the border between Buganda and Bugangaizi. Kikukule did not come from the established ruling families. He was Kabalega's creation. In 1893, he was detailed to defend the Kafu River area. He confronted Major Owen, a British officer and engaged him for "...a good three hours of hard fighting".[9]

Then there was General Ireta Byangome whose base was at Mboga (now part of the Democratic Republic of Congo). He was charged with the defence of that border. Ireta was a Munyankole by birth and belonged to the Musaigi clan. He was the one who led that disastrous campaign from Ankole against Kabalega during the succession war. He was captured and then joined Kabalega's army. He is said to have been a faithful servant of the crown up to the very end. Thereafter, he moved to Kasagama's Toro.

The Omukama was able to equip his army because the Bunyoro-Kitara of the time, unlike the present "Bunyoro", was one of the wealthiest areas of present Uganda. The main source of wealth was ivory. Bunyoro had also established business contact with Arab traders.

The Kingdom had accumulated sufficient funds to maintain a well-equipped regular army with a large reserve force. Such was the military climate of Bunyoro-Kitara when the British intruders appeared on the scene.

Kabalega's first battle with the foreign intruders was in June 1872. It was after Baker purported to have taken formal possession of Bunyoro in the name of the Khedive of Egypt. The Khedive's intention was to found an empire over the equator so as to control the waters of the Nile upon which the people of Egypt depend on and continue to do so ever so much. At first, Kabalega had hoped that he had found an ally in Baker, but Baker's behaviour soon prompted Kabalega and his people to expel the intruder after setting Kabalega's temporary camp at Masindi ablaze. Baker ran for his dear life across the Nile. The battle of Masindi is locally known as Baligota-Isansa, (Because Baker's fort was besieged long after he had escaped). Meanwhile, the Omukama moved from Masindi to Mparo near Hoima from where he sent armies between 1872 to 1876 to reconquer Butuku, Toro and Bukonjo, which had rebelled in 1830 during the reign

9   *Parl Papers, Africa No 7 (1895)*

of his great grandfather. He managed to regain control of Busongora, Bwamba, Buziba, Bulega and Mboga. Kabalega remained in full control of Butuku, Toro, and Bukonjo until late in 1891. Kabalega's remains were laid to rest at Mparo, which today is one of the tourist attractions in Uganda.

Kabalega's second encounter was with Henry Morton Stanley who was on his journey across Africa. The battle took place at the Buruli crossing of River Kafu. It became clear that Kabalega was impeding communication lines between Khartoum and Lake Victoria. The British administrators and their agents from Sudan often came into conflict with Kabalega and his people when making journeys to Lake Victoria and vice-versa.

After several minor skirmishes it was thought necessary to come to terms with Bunyoro-Kitara. Emin pasha was dispatched to initiate a dialogue in 1877. What Emin Pasha found at Mparo (near Hoima) is amply described by A.R. Dunbar in one of *Uganda's Famous Men* Series: *Omukama Chwa 11, Kabalega* (East African Literature Bureau 1965) p13: "At Mparo, Emin found a market containing a collection of the most diverse products and a crowd containing the representatives of nearly all the tribes in Eastern Equatorial Africa. The unit of currency was the cowry shell, 500 of which were equivalent to the Maria Theresa thaler. Trade in Bunyoro-Kitara had depended upon Buganda because Mutesa would not allow the Arabs to go from Buganda to Bunyoro. It was much to his advantage to claim possession of all firearms and ammunition brought by the Arabs as trade goods. As a result, neither Kamurasi nor Kabalega had been in a position to retaliate for the raids made upon them by Buganda. Despite the ban, two enterprising Arabs had reached Bunyoro in 1872 and in return for presenting half their trade goods, including arms and ammunition to Kabalega, they obtained accommodation, food and five times the value of the goods in ivory. Thus Kabalega was no longer at a disadvantage. There was an export trade in coffee, bark cloth, hides, salt, pottery, iron, mats, fruits resins and wood. When Emin Pasha came face to face with the Omukama for the first time, Kabalega was dressed in a piece of fine orange-pink coloured bark cloth. It covered his body to his breast except for the left-hand shoulder, over which was thrown a piece of darker coloured bark cloth. He wore a necklace of hairs from a giraffe's tail, the middle of which was strung a single blue glass bead, which encircled his neck. He was strikingly fair and about five feet, ten inches tall. He made a most favourable impression on Emin Pasha.

Emin spent over two months in Bunyoro and met the Omukama several times. Because Emin spoke Arabic, he was able to communicate direct with Kabalega..." Emin made friends with the Omukama and the two men agreed on certain terms designed to create mutual trust and confidence. The result of this agreement was that for the next eighteen months there was great understanding between the Banyoro and Egyptians administrators. Access by white travellers became easy. This gave Kabalega and his people a free hand to concentrate on the administration of the kingdom.

Following the understanding with Emin Pasha, Kabalega returned to the mission closest to his heart, which was to reunite the kingdom of Bunyoro-Kitara and regain its past glory. The Kingdom had suffered a set back during the reign of his two immediate predecessors. Within a short period he was able to dethrone Kasagama whom he regarded as an imposter. Kasagama had been installed as king of Toro by Captain Lugard sometime in 1891. He was driven into the foothills of Rwenzori Mountains by two of Kabalega's ablest military commanders. They were Ireta and Rwabudongo referred to above. Meanwhile, two British military officers who were bent on a showdown with Bunyoro appeared on the scene in the persons of Major Macdonald and Colonel Colvile. The main invasion of Bunyoro-Kitara was launched on New Year's Eve of 1893. Kabalega opened three fronts. He sent an army to Busongora under Kikukule to face the Sudanese troops who were stationed there by the colonial military leaders. He stationed a permanent contingent of men in Bugerere. Kikukule in Toro did not offer much resistance. He quickly retreated and joined Kabalega at the border with Buganda. It was at that point where Colonel Colvile's men were concentrated under the command of Kakungulu. It is said there were eight European officers, four hundred Sudanese and 15,000 'Ganda' troops. Apparently there was little resistance at this point. Kabalega's army withdrew and opted for a guerilla type of war that lasted for four years. Fierce battles did take place during that protracted war because the entire kingdom of Bunyoro-Kitara remained defiant even after the capture and defeat of the Omukama Kabalega, as will be explained later. For the moment, let us recall the words of Jackson, one of the early British agents, who acknowledges, "After Kabalega had been driven from his capital and was a fugitive, he kept together a sufficiently large force to put up several stiff fights and to the very last was a nasty thorn in our side":[10]

It is of great significance to note that the Banyoro and King Kabalega were not alone in their resolve to resist foreign rule. Kabaka Mwanga of Buganda joined them. As already stated when Mwanga, who had been

10   F. Jackson, *Early Days in East Africa* (London, 1930) p274.

detained by the Germans in Tanganyika (now Tanzania) reappeared in Masaka, which was part of his kingdom, he was able to attract a considerable following. The colonial military pursued him without avail. He got away and joined Kabalega, who had again taken the field in northern Bunyoro and then provided a rallying point for the dissident Sudanese troops. Somewhere in Igara, what is today part of Bushenyi district, the king of Igara decided to commit suicide. His neighbour, the king of Kajara, withdrew to Tanganyika. In Busoga cooperation was won only by threatening the rulers with disposition and deportation.

To return to the Omukama Kabalega, he crossed the Nile and spent about two years in Aduku Lango. From there he continued to harass the British across the river until April 9, 1899 where by the edge of a swamp, the Omukama Kabalega Chwa II of Bunyoro Kitara with some of his sons and a few soldiers of his bodyguard were taken by surprise by his British-led pursuers. Even at that time when he knew the end had come, he put up a gallant fight, killing and wounding many of the Indian, Swahili, Sudanese and Ganda troops. "When seized the Omukama was with Kabaka Mwanga of Buganda who by 1897 had also rejected alien rule. Those two Kings, Chwa II of Bunyoro Kitara and Mwanga II of Buganda were nationalists who preferred the honour of battle to acquiescence in indignities of imperial control," says J.H. Mittelman, *Ideology and Politics in Uganda 1975*, p89. Both Mwanga and Kabalega desired peace with honour and had no wish to compromise the independence of their kingdoms. An overwhelming number of Ugandans today share that view.

I have chosen to highlight the gallant resistance staged against colonialism by Kabaka Mwanga and Omukama Kabalega and other gallant sons of the soil to dispel once and for all the mistaken belief that the people of Uganda were oblivious to acts of aggression perpetrated against them by the early imperialists and their agents. As a matter of fact, there were uprisings against the intruders of whatever description throughout the length and breadth of the country. Elders tell us about these matters-true details are scanty, but we know that the Bakiga, for instance, took up arms in 1914 -15, the Alur and the Madi of West Nile fought fierce battles. The Acholi, the Langi ,and the Iteso Staged the Lamagi Rebellion in 1911-12.

It is imperative and appropriate to put on record that not all the people in this country were willing to forego their liberty or exchange their freedom for servitude under the British without a fight. Ugandans today in search of their roots attach great importance to our forefathers and all those people who, in one way or another, put up gallant and dignified resistance against both European and Arab invaders in an effort to preserve our freedom and identity. It was through that early resistance that the seed of nationalism was sown. This seed was later to re-germinate and flourish. It gave impetus to the organised nationalism of the 1950s described in this work. This assertion will undoubtedly raise some controversy among many Ugandans. If a controversy does indeed arise, it will be a sign of self- realisation. For the moment, I can only say that it is high time to decolonise the history of Uganda and indeed the entire continent of Africa. Let Africans speak for themselves.

Chapter Three

Economic History Of Uganda

It will be recalled that Uganda's economic development during the 1960s was propelled by a vibrant export drive based on cotton and coffee. The two crops were grown by peasant farmers and processed by indigenous Ugandans through co-operative Growers Unions. Copper, tea, hides and skins and a wide range of manufactured products supplemented the coffee and cotton exports.

Tourism had also developed into a major foreign exchange earner. Uganda Hotels under the Uganda Development Corporation played a decisive role in the development of tourism. Major development projects were initiated throughout the country by state-owned enterprises in collaboration with some private investors. Uganda boasted of a strong currency, a balanced budget, low taxes and price stability. The good economic performance was due to sound fiscal and monetary policies enunciated by the government of the day. The vibrant economy provided employment opportunities for school leavers, university graduates etc. The brain drain of trained and skilled manpower to foreign lands to seek green pastures was unknown. Suddenly, there was a dramatic change when Idi Amin, in conjunction with imperialist agents, staged a military coup and took over the reigns of power. He declared an economic war that brought the country's economy to ruins.

The second UPC government, commonly known as "Obote II", put in place a Recovery Programme 1981-85. The government committed itself to reversing the decline of the Amin era. Bold economic and financial policies, strategies and measures were adopted from 1981 with the objective of stimulating production and restoring economic stability. The highlights of success following implementation of these measures were:

- Economic recovery began to be recorded right from the end of 1981, intensifying in 1984, with Real Gross National Product (GNP) reaching a new peak of shs 7,582 billion in 1984, approximately, 0.5% higher than it had been in 1972. (*Background to The Budget 1985/86*).

- Real Gross Domestic Product (GDP) increased over the years from 1981 through to 1983, registering a growth of 7.3% in 1983 over the 1982 figure. Given the national population growth rate of about 3% then, this represented a rise in per capita income of 4.3%. The total GDP, at 1966 prices, went up by 5.2% in 1984 compared with the 1983 growth of 4.9% while per capita income rose by over 2.3% over the 1983 level. (*Background to the Budget 1984/85*).

- Inflation was drastically reduced from 104% in 1981 to between 25% and 30% in 1983/84 although drought, declining export earnings and debt-service costs again caused a marked increase in inflation in the first half of 1984/85.

- Marked coffee production hit a new high of 135,000 tons representing an increase of 3% over the period, inspite of reduction of Uganda's coffee quota in the international market.

- Lint cotton production drastically increased from a mere 6,000 tons in 1982 to 12,000 tons in 1984, yielding 100% increase.

- Tea production increased from 1,700 tons in 1981 to 5,500 tons in 1985, inspite of limited external funding. Tobacco production increased from 63 tons in 1981 to 1,959 tons, despite NRM inspired insurgency around tobacco growing areas (West Nile, Masindi, Hoima and Mubende districts).

- Producer prices were increased from time to time as an incentive for increased production. (see, *Statistics Department, Ministry of Planning and Economic Development*).

- Despite NRA's bush war tactics to scare away tourists, there was a steady increase in the number of tourists coming to Uganda. In 1983 for instance, there were 13,000 tourist visitors up from 10,000 in 1982. Modest construction and rehabilitation of hotels especially around Kampala began.

- Balance of payments deficits of 1981 were progressively reduced until converted to positive in 1984.
- Performance of the economy during 1984/85 was on the whole satisfactory, despite the adverse international and domestic factors. Recurrent revenue rose by shs 22 billion from shs 134 billion to shs 156 billion. Development revenue rose by shs 4 billion from shs 53 billion to shs 57 billion. This positive increase was due to higher exchange rate, but did not represent the realisation in dollar terms of external grants and loans, which were meant to bring the budgeted shs 53 billion. During the year the total amount disbursed was US $110 million against the budget figure of shs $160.6 million from external grants and loans (see, *Bank of Uganda*).

But the economic gains achieved by the government were messed up and lost following General Lutwa's coup of July 27, 1985. As the country's economy was beginning to pick up and stabilise, the enemies of peaceful progress and stability became restless. Their greatest fear was that unless something drastic took place early 1985, President Milton Obote would call general elections and his party would win another term of five years. Hence, the intensification of insurgency in the Luwero Triangle that ignited an orchestrated international outcry over human rights abuse and called on the major donor countries to cut down on aid and financing. When the intensified insurgency appeared to be failing, General Tito Okello staged an externally inspired military coup in July of that year.

The coup brought an abrupt end to the economic success story, as exemplified in the attached data. It is worth pondering that the same international donor community that condemned the "atrocities" in the Luwero Triangle seventeen years earlier was oblivious of the heinous crimes that have been committed and continued to be committed against the people of Northern Uganda since 1986. Is it a question of double standards or simply a matter of being caught up in a web of one's own creation?

Privatisation

By 1987 the economic situation had become intractable mainly due to the naivety and ineptitude of the new regime. The NRM initially refused bluntly to have anything to do with the Recovery Programme and the major funding contributors to the programme, that is to say, the World Bank and the International Monetary Fund (IMF). NRM intransigence had nothing to do with the economic policy. It was due to misguided politics. Museveni's personal obsession with Obote was a big factor in the uncompromising attitude towards the World Bank and the International Monetary Fund (IMF). He accused former president of selling out to the two international bodies. Because politics in Uganda is perceived as revolving around personalities, the NRM put aside national interests and succumbed to the politics of personality cult.

It is advisable that future leaders pay heed to the words of Alexander Pope: "Virtous and vicious every man must be, few in extreme, but all in the degree." (*Essay on Man*, (1733). Be that as it may, the regime toyed with the idea of pursuing the discredited and out-moded communist policies –policies which had no place in the Recovery Programme as the ideology of 'Moving to the Left' had tactfully been abandoned. Times and world trends had changed.

For almost eighteen months the regime indulged in the exercise of trial and error. A host of economic policies that exposed their immaturity, ineptitude and complete inability to manage the national economy were pronounced. They tried to distribute essential commodities in order to combat scarcity of goods, stationed armed guards to stop smuggling at Uganda borders with neigbhouring countries. Inspired by communist countries like Cuba, they attempted barter trade. The nation and the world looked on with utter amazement. The barter trade policy left social ripples. The regime ordered farmers to grow maize, beans and other crops but failed to find a market for the produce. Farmers lost colossal amounts of money in revenue. The Mityana-Fort Portal road, which was to be constructed on the basis of barter bears testimony to the naïve and ill-conceived policy of the so-called 'integrated and self-sustainable' economy.

There was a currency reform in May 1987. Two zeros were deleted from the value of the currency in circulation. To complete the exercise a currency conversion tax of 30% was imposed supposedly as development tax. Accountability for that tax has never been given. All in all, the impact on people's financial standing was staggering. As if that was not enough, a bank interest of 40% was imposed. To most enlightened Ugandans the currency reform remains a genesis of abject poverty that has hit the majority of the population for so long.

Suddenly, the regime made a complete U-turn with gusto and has since blindly embraced the World Bank and IMF doctrines. Thereafter,

NRM embarked on fullscale privatisation and liberalisation without due regard to the plight of the majority of the citizens. That now the cold war is no more, 'free enterprise' and 'market forces' are in the forefront of economic aid. Divestiture is on the lips of everybody who matters in the Third World because the donor countries through their powerful aid agents have decreed that it should be so. Leaders of the Third World must appear to be progressive and modern despite their economic handicaps.

In the words of Graham Hancock, "If conservative values are enjoying a resurgence on the other hand, then notions like 'structural adjustment' will be promulgated, the virtue of private enterprise will be extolled and market forces will be assigned a god like omnipotence". He concludes: "Indeed the truth is that notions of how aid should be used to promote development have since the 1940s, been at least as subject to the whims of fashion as the length of men's hair or the hemlines of women's skirts" (Hancock,1989, 71-73). So, divestiture is just a fad. What is important is to inquire how the Ugandan government has reacted to the current fad in the aid industry? The whole country has been transformed into a huge auction mart. National assets in the form of government-owned enterprises are disposed of indiscriminately under the banner "We must sell now". The NRM government has taken full advantage of the privatisation process to distribute political rewards and privileges to individual supporters of the movement in disregard of economic benefits to the country. But even if the sale was conducted on a competitive basis in the spirit of market forces, it is hard to imagine that indigenous Ugandans could compete effectively in the race to buy government-owned enterprises. The African is pitted against unfair competition with foreigners and local Asian businessmen. It is a fact that the majority of Ugandans have been economically incapacitated over the years. They do not have capital and have no access to credit facilities.

That is why during the post-independence era it was expedient for countries emerging from colonial rule, including Uganda, to set up their own mode of development. The mode was neither communistic nor capitalistic. It was a national economic policy designed to stimulate development and to put in place an equitable way of distributing the fruits of indepence. Because trade and commerce had been for a long time a preserve of foreigners and non-indigenous Ugandans the immediate post-independence government established key commercial institutions to correct the imbalance. Accordingly, the Uganda Commercial Bank and the Marketing Boards for Uganda's major export crops were strengthened and expanded. The Uganda Commercial Bank was the only bank that

Ugandans could call their own and it had branches throughout the country.

The dubious and scandalous way the bank was disposed of smacks of criminal opportunism. With the sale of the Coffee and Produce Marketing Boards, the farmers were left at the mercy of unscrupulous produce dealers. The quality of Uganda coffee once the envy of international coffee roasters has deteriorated. Farmers of minor crops like maize and beans were getting peanuts for their produce. Why–because the change was so sudden. There was no adequate preparation for the changeover. A system of local monopolies was developing. Many local businessmen and women who rushed into the market found themselves greatly restricted by lack of capital. As Joseph Stiglitz puts it: "It takes capital and entrepreneurship to create new firms and jobs, and in the developing countries there is often a shortage of the latter due to lack of education and of the former due to lack of bank financing." (Stiglitz, 2003, 59).

With the sale of the Uganda Commercial Bank and the deliberate destruction of the Cooperative Bank, small and medium local businesses had no access to credit facilities. Foreign-owned banks patronised only big businesses and the few surviving local banks were not in position to compete with them.

The dangers of relying on foreign banks have been manifested in many countries. Argentina is the latest victim and yet the government of Uganda remains completely oblivious of such dangers.

The worst is yet to come. Government is under pressure from the World Bank and the IMF to privatise infrastructures and essential services. The Uganda Elecetricity board has already been privatised and the National Water and Sewerage Corporation charged with the responsibility of providing safe and clean water to the population is under threat and so is the Uganda Railways Corporation. Most African governments are reluctant to privatise public utilities out of fear that unlike in the developed countries where privatisation of such utilities ushers in competition, in Africa it is just a matter of replacing a parastatal body with a private firm. The assumption is that an average private firm will be more efficient than a state-owned enterprise. The sale of the Uganda Electricity Board has not yet proved that assumption to be correct. As a matter of fact, the only visible change is the increased tariff rates! Power cuts or failures are commonplace.

The primary and fundamental function of any caring government is to harness the natural resources of the country for economic and social advancement of its citizens. This is the precept that ought to have guided the NRM government in its pursuit of divestiture policy. Thousands of civil servants were retrenched and soldiers demobilised without adequate terminal packages. The entire exercise was a national disaster punctuated by nepotism, cronism and sheer corruption. In the circumstances the options would have been to introduce contract management for selected enterprises and sell shares of other parastatals to members of the public. Nobody doubts that Ugandans are the ultimate owners of the parastatals because it was the tax-payer who provided the initial capital investment. Ugandans reserve the right to revisit the entire process of divestiture at an appropriate time.

Conventional wisdom dictates that economic liberalisation must be accompanied by political freedom. Political freedom, it must be emphasised, fosters good governance, stability and creativity. Economic development must be linked to political pluralism, if the fight against corruption, nepotism, military dictatorship is to be meaningful and successful. It must also be realised that genuine economic development that will raise the standard of living and improve the quality of life in Uganda must be based on self-help and domestic savings to accumulate the necessary capital. To do that Ugandans must first regain their lost confidence and political leadership must restore respect for national sovereignty.

Breaking from Foreign Aid and the Dependency Syndrome

Freedom fighters, who struggled and fought for independence in various parts of Africa, had a great vision for the continent and a deep insight for the aspirations of the African people. That is why after a substantial number of African countries had attained independence African leaders went right ahead and established new institutions to express a new sense of unity. The institutions included the Organisation of African Unity (OAU), the Economic Commission for Africa (ECA), the African Development Bank ((ADB) and a number of sub-region economic groupings. The Charter of OAU signed on May 25, 1963 declared, inter alia, that it was the inalienable right of all people to control their destiny and that freedom, equality, justice and dignity were essential objectives of the African peoples. Most important, the Charter pledged to harness the natural and human resources of Africa for total advancement of Africans. It is the latter part of that declaration that must preoccupy the minds of the people and governments of Africa today.

Chapter Four

Political Reforms Leading To Independence

A great event took place in November 1958. Sir Frederick Crawford, the governor, announced in the Legislative Council the appointment and terms of reference of a constitutional committee. One of the terms of reference proved to be very controversial. That was 'to consider and to recommend to the governor the form of direct elections on a common roll for representatives of the Legislative Council to be introduced in 1961'. The controversy split the UNC into two irreconcilable factions. One of the factions advocated separate voters' registers, one for the Africans and another for the non-Africans (Europeans and Asians). Another faction wanted common voters' register. The latter group was headed by A.M. Obote and had the support of four UNC elected members. The anti-common roll was headed by J.W. Kiwanuka and Dr. B.N. Kununka, who were not members of LEGCO. Every effort to reconcile their differences failed. The rift became permanent. The Kiwanuka – Kununka faction slowly but surely passed into oblivion.

In the meantime, the independent elected members of LEGCO who had previously been members of UNC formed a new political party, the Uganda Peoples' Union. The leadership of the new party was mainly from the Western Region. This could probably be considered to have been the first signal for an ethnic divide which was to play a dubious and dangerous role in the politics of the late 1980s and 1990s under the National Resistance Movement. Contrary to expectation, the NRM government has widened the ethnic divide between the Southern Bantu and the Northern Nilotics.

In order to implement the governor's announcement of November 1958, a constitutional committee[11] was appointed.

It was during the course of the Constitutional Committee enquiry that Obote's faction of UNC took the initiative to have a dialogue with members of the Legislative Council who had drifted away from the parent party (UNC) with a view to getting them back to the fold. Those members as we have seen had banded together in December 1958 to form a new party, the Uganda People's Union (UPU). Milton Obote did not stop there. He approached one of the African ministers to convene a meeting of all political parties in the country. There were about half a dozen major political parties in the country, namely, the Uganda National Congress, Democratic Party, Progressive Party, United Congress Party led by E. Muwazi and the Uganda Peoples Union. The objective was to form a united front in backing certain strategic submissions to the committee that could accelerate the advent of independence. It turned out that only three political parties were invited to take part in the meeting i.e. the DP, UPU and the two camps of UNC. The parties considered the proposal for a merger but failed to agree on how best to implement it. Benedicto Kiwanuka of DP adopted an uncompromising attitude. He could not hear of dissolving the DP, he would rather see the DP swallow the other parties. The effort proved futile. However, in January 1960 members of the other negotiating parties, that is, UNC lead by A.M. Obote and Abubakar Mayanja and the newly formed UPU agreed in principle to merge. Thereafter, both parties carried out consultations with their respective executive committees to formalise the merger. A public announcement to that effect was made in March 1960. The new party assumed the name of Uganda Peoples Congress. The merger was preceded by the publication of the Wild Committee Report, which recommended direct elections on a Common Roll in all districts based on universal adult suffrage. The committee was divided on the constitution of the Legislative Council and the Executive Council. The majority advocated an immediate move to internal self-government after the 1961 elections with a chief minister and a council of ministers drawn from and responsible to the Legislature. It, however, recommended that three ex official ministers, namely, the Chief Secretary, the Attorney General and the Minister of Finance should be retained. The three were

11   Members of the committee were:
J.V. Wild, O.B.E. – Chairman;A.A. Baerlein C.B.E.;J.B. Bazarabusa, M.B.E.;K. Ingham, M..C.;H.K. Jaffer, C.B.E.;C.B. Katiti;Erisa Kironde;B.K. Kirya;G.B.K. Magezi;B. Mukasa, O.B.E.;W.W. Kajumbula-Nadiope;A.M. Obote;C.J. Obwangor;G Oda;C.K. Patel, C.B.E., Q.C.;F.K. Kalimuzo, Secretary

expatriate officials. The minority proposed that the appointment of the Chief Minister be deferred and that the Executive Council should continue to be advisory to the Governor. The recommendations of the majority reflected the views of the UPC, which continued to press for the demand 'Independence Now' enunciated by the UNC.

By the time of the election campaign all major political parties were demanding immediate self-government. However, there was one lonely but powerful voice of dissent, Buganda, which had earlier on refused either to nominate a representative to the Wild Committee or to give evidence. Buganda's argument was that there should be no further political or constitutional changes until and after her status and the position of Kabaka had been resolved.

The publication of the Constitutional Committee Report brought to the forefront the conflict between the political parties and the Mengo establishment. The political parties stood for attainment of self-government in the shortest possible time for Uganda as a unitary state. The Mengo establishment remained adamant and continued to agitate for a federal structure with special safeguards for the Kingdom of Buganda. It was with that background that in February 1960 the colonial administration made a public announcement that elections would be held in early 1961. The colonial office also gave assurances that the country would not move to self-government immediately after the elections. The assurances were welcomed not only by Buganda but by all the Kingdoms. The elections announcement was followed by a three prong strategy to ensure an organised and peaceful handing over of state power.

- The General elections would be held as scheduled.
- A commission would be appointed to consider the future form of government for Uganda.
- A conference, consisting of representatives of all districts, Buganda, political parties and other interest groups would be convened in London to consider the future form of government.
- The terms of reference for the commission were:

To consider the future form of government best suited to Uganda and the question of the relationship between the central government and the other authorities in Uganda, bearing in mind:

- Her Majesty's government known resolve to lead Uganda by appropriate stages to independence and to this end to develop stable institutions of government which will properly reflect the particular circumstances and meet the needs of Uganda, and

- The desire of the peoples of Uganda to preserve their existing institutions and customs and the status and dignity of their rulers and leaders.
- The special relationship that already exists between Her Majesty's government and His Highness the Kabaka's government and the native governments of Bunyoro, Ankole and Toro as set down in the various agreements that have been made with the traditional rulers and peoples of Buganda, Bunyoro, Ankole and Toro and to make recommendations.

The strategy devised by the British government went a very long way in bringing together representatives of the people of Uganda drawn from every social sector to a Round Table to discuss and to find a resolution to outstanding issues that threatened to retard progress towards independence. The London conference provided a breathing space for political rivals. It is a great tribute to the participants, who were able, to a certain extent to forget their petty quarrels and rise to the occasion. It was at this juncture that political activity was intensified. There was a great deal of political alignment and realignment of ethnic and religious groupings.

However, the formation of the Uganda Peoples Congress was not well received in Buganda because the merger was seen as a deliberate move to isolate the central region. The immediate reaction in Buganda was to form the Uganda National Movement ostensibly to champion and advance the cause of Africans in trade and commerce. It was a visible sign that Buganda was opposed to activities of political parties in its Kingdom. The publication of the Wild Committee Report left no shadow of doubt in the minds of politicians and the population at large that Uganda was destined for big changes in the future. Dan. M. Mudola describes the mood as follows, "It was obvious that colonialism in Uganda was at its nadir and new men had to be found to accede to power"[12] It is probably safe to say that out of the race for power was born the Uganda Peoples Congress for those who had abandoned the UNC deemed it prudent to return to the fold. The emergence of the UPC on the political scene of Uganda precipitated two reactions, a direct confrontation between the tribal traditionalists and the nationalists. The other dimension was the resurrection of the religious rivalry experienced in the late 19th century

12   *Religion, Ethnicity and Politics in Uganda* (Fountain Publishers, Kampala, Uganda) p21.

between Protestants and Catholics. It was a pathetic situation for the young generation that strongly believed in creating a modern secular state in Uganda. Ethnicity and religion became ingredients of Uganda politics – a trend that continues to bedevil Ugandan politics. There were two major political parties in the field, the Uganda Peoples Congress and the Democratic Party. The DP was dubbed a party for Catholics and the UPC passed for Protestants. There was justification for the religious labels in both cases. James H. Mittelman, puts it this way, "Benedicto Kiwanuka's Democratic Party (DP) established in 1954 as an antineo-traditional party, tended to attract Catholic members, in contrast to UPC which, despite the Catholics among its leaders, derived its backing largely from the Protestant community": *Ideology and Politics in Uganda*, 1975, p72. In fairness, he ought to have added that even the Democratic Party had outstanding Protestants as members of the Executive Committee, viz. Balamu Mukasa, former Katikiro of Bunyoro, and Stanley Bemba, former Clerk Assistant to the Legislative Council.

As we have seen the Protectorate Government accepted most of the Committee's recommendations. In February 1960, the Governor announced that elections would take place early in 1961 and that no radical changes would follow immediately. The announcement did not please the political parties because self-government would not follow immediately after the elections while the Mengo clique was horrified by the prospect of having an almost wholly elected legislature before the future form of government was agreed upon and safeguards for Buganda's position in an independent Uganda secured. In response to the announcement the Buganda Lukiko sent a memorandum to Her Majesty the Queen in which a demand for BUGANDA's independence was made. As expected the demand was rejected. Buganda threatened to secede by January 1st 1961. The demands were futile and the declaration came to nothing. Plans for elections went ahead. However, it must be pointed out that due to the uncompromising attitude of the Kabaka's government the registration of voters in Buganda was poor. About 700,000 people in Buganda were qualified to register as voters but only 35,000 people managed to register. In the rest of the country the registration was a success recording 75 per cent.

The general elections took place as scheduled and were contested by five political parties, namely, the Uganda Peoples Congress, the Democratic Party, the Uganda National Congress, the Uganda Hereditary Chieftainship Party and the Uganda African Union. Out of the five parties only two, namely, the Uganda Peoples' Congress and the Democratic Party, commanded wide support.

At the close of the poll, the Democratic Party came out victorious. The DP victory was attributed to its overwhelming support in Buganda, the boycott and the intimidation, not withstanding. It managed to "win" all the 21 seats in Buganda. The Uganda Peoples Congress was second because it had a great following outside Buganda. It polled a total of 488 334 votes as against DP's 407 461. The final state of the parties was as follows: DP 43, UPC 35, UNC 1 and Independents 2. The Democratic Party under the leadership of Benedicto Kiwanuka was called upon to form a new administration. The new Legislative Council consisted of the Speaker, Sir John Griffin, three ex-official members: the Chief Secretary, the Attorney General and the Financial Secretary, eighty two directly elected members of the council, bringing the total membership to one hundred and two.

[13]Members of the Council of Ministers as it was then known were:

Leader of Government Business:	B.K.M. Kiwanuka
Minister of Legal Affairs:	R. L. E. Dreschfield, CMG, QC.
Minister of Finance:	C.G.F.F. Melmouth, CMG
Minister of Security & External Affairs:	C. Powel Cotton, CMG, MBE, MC.
Minister of Education:	J.C. Kiwanuka
Minister of Economic Development:	L. Sebalu
Minister of Health:	D. J.K. Nabeta
Minister of Local Government:	B.K. Bataringaya
Minister of Works:	N.E. Opio
Minister of Agricultural & Animal Industry:	B.J. Mukasa
Minister of Land & Water Resources:	Matayo Mugwanya
Minister of Social Development & Labour:	Stanley Bemba
Ministry of Commerce & Industry:	C.K. Patel

There were eight parliamentary secretaries to assist the ministers in the execution of their duties. Paul Kawanga Semogerere was one of them. He was later to take over the mantle of the party's leadership after the liberation war of 1979. It is to be noted that colonial administrators referred to as ex-official members held the three key portfolios of Finance, Legal Affairs and Security. In effect that meant the leader of government business held virtually no executive powers. His main schedule was to co-ordinate government business in the Legislative Council. It was a very trying position for him because he had not served before as member of

13   *HANSARD.. Second Meeting, 41ˢᵗ session, November 1961.*

the council. It was a position that kept him in the public eye and made him the main target for attacks from the opposition. His performance in this role exposed him most. In the first instance, the majority members of his team did not have previous experience either in government or in the council. The inexperienced ministers were pitted against a determined and formidable opposition composed of men who had been in the council for a considerable period of time. They had picked up the minute intricacies of parliamentary procedure and felt confident on the floor of the council. The outstanding personalities were, among others: A.M Obote, J.K. Babiiha, G.B.K. Magezi, C.J. Obwangor, G.S. Ibingira and J.B.T. Kakonge. At that time the standing orders and rules of procedure were almost identical with those of the House of Commons – the mother of parliaments, with all the unwritten conventions that go with them.

For instance, everyday of the week during the session of the Council, one hour was devoted to a simple but important item on the Agenda or Order of Business- 'Parliamentary Questions'. While the basic function of any legislature is to make laws for peace, order and good government of the country, Legislature need to be kept informed of what different branches of government are doing. They need to assess and evaluate the performance of government. They also need opportunities to air their grievances in respect of any government policy. The simplest and most cost effective device was to allow backbenchers and opposition members to raise in the Council any matter for which government bore responsibility. The procedure was that a member desiring basic information would submit the question in writing to the office of the Clerk of Council. The Clerk of Council was the Chief Executive officer responsible for the administration of the Council. The designation has nothing to do with clerical work. He was and still is the Chief Administrator of the Administrative Department in Parliament. The title is derived from the mode of work employed in the early days of Parliament. To return to the parliamentary questions, officials of the council would vet and verify each and every question and decide whether or not it was admissible. More often than not the officials had to rephrase the text of the question and to render it consistent with parliamentary language. After that, the question would be forwarded to the appropriate Minister responsible for the matter being raised. It was then incumbent on the Minister or indeed the government to furnish the information sought any time after the lapse of two days unless directed otherwise. On the appointed day the question would be placed on the order of business with a panel member. All that the questioner had to do was to stand up when called upon to do so by the speaker and say "Mr. Speaker, Question no so and so standing in my name". The verbal fireworks would then begin especially when the reply given was considered unsatisfactory. A barrage of supplementary questions (unwritten) would follow.

The exchange between the Minister and the members fascinated the public. By and large the way a minister was able to dispose of the question gave some measure of his ability or degree of performance. This is where most of Kiwanuka' ministers failed him. They did not show their wits. They failed to deliver. To a lesser extent this was true of even parliamentary debates on bills, resolutions and of course the budget. The opposition very often had a field day. That did not help the government to promote a good image. Indeed, it can be said that it eroded their credibility. One incident comes to mind. In November 1961, the Member for Bunyoro South West moved a motion on the "Lost Counties" in which he was urging the British government to organise a referendum to assess the inhabitants" views. During the course of the debate the Leader of the Government Business asserted that the Mover of the motion was present at the London conference when that issue was discussed and that he did not raise a finger. So, he had no moral justification to re-open debate on that issue. It, however, transpired that actually the Mover of the motion was not physically in London at the material time. It was a regrettable blunder. The opposition exploited the situation to the maximum by ridiculing the Chief Minister and Leader of government business. There were many such incidents.

It must be pointed out that question time continued to be a source of attraction after independence. The position was reversed. Members of the DP moved to the Opposition. It was their turn to keep members on the Front Bench (Ministers) on their toes. The most active Opposition members in this respect were Martin Okello, J.Obonyo, Boniface Byanyima, A.A.Latim, G. O. Oda and of course the Leader of Opposition, Basil Bataringaya.

The Democratic Party as, stated earlier, was born out of frustration perpetrated by the Mengo Protestant hegemony against Catholics in Buganda. The Leader of the Democratic Party, Benedicto Kiwanuka, could not conceal his aversion to the Mengo establishment. Once in government he lost no time in throwing his weight about in an attempt to assert his authority. He became arrogant especially in his public statements on the position of the Kabaka in an independent Uganda. This is what James H. Mittelman has to say in this regard, " … issues within Buganda became polarised in terms of Kiwanuka versus the Kabaka, and for the average Muganda it was heresy to conceive of a peasant holding a position above the traditional leader. This inherent difficulty with Buganda was aggravated by Kiwanuka's abrasive personality and his penchant for employing inflammatory tactics"[14] The British came to the aid of Mengo. In order to allay Mengo's fear they renewed the assurances that Her Majesty's government was determined to safeguard the position of hereditary rulers. The assurances were reflected in the Terms of Reference of the Munster Commission. The Commission came out with, inter-alia, three important recommendations:

- that Buganda's relationship with Uganda should be federal,
- that the Kabaka should become a genuine constitutional monarch and withdrawal from politics
- and more important – a directly elected Lukiko, if it so wished, could choose to act as an electoral college to elect the representatives from Buganda to the National Assembly.

That effectively sealed Kiwanuka's political aspiration. At the same time his relations with the top colonial civil servants deteriorated by the day, following his threat to expel British expatriates after independence. To prove his point he despatched three hundred young Ugandans for overseas studies in preparation for the intended expulsion. The colonial administration in Kampala and the colonial office in London did not take kindly to Kiwanuka's utterances and actions. The colonial administrators hardened their attitude against Kiwanuka. They were happy to see him go. That was the state of affairs when the First Independence Constitutional Conference opened at Lancaster House in London in September 1961. The main participants were:

- the British government which, strange as it may sound, assumed the role of an honest broker;
- the Buganda government;
- the three Kingdoms of Bunyoro, Ankole and Toro and the Territory of Busoga;
- the non-kingdom districts;
- and last, but not least, the aspiring successors to the colonial authority, the Uganda Peoples Congress and the Democratic Party.

The demands and the interests of the contending groups may be briefly summarised as follows:

14   *Ideology and Politics in Uganda 1975* (P73).

Buganda's desire was to secure a federal form of government which accorded a special position to the Kingdom of Buganda and constitutional safeguards entrenching the status of the Kabaka. Determined to emulate Buganda, the Western Region kingdoms also demanded federal status and safeguards for their hereditary rulers. Busoga demanded similar treatment. The people in the rest of the country placed their confidence and hope in the political institutions at the Centre. It goes without saying that the two political parties' major interest was to gain power from Britain. The UPC target was to wrestle power from the ruling Democratic Party, while the latter's pre-occupation was to retain that power. The Democratic Party's strategy at the conference was to appear as the foremost champion of undiluted democracy by advocating direct elections at all levels throughout the country. The UPC, on the other hand, chose to be more cautious. Aware of the situation on the ground the UPC conceded Buganda's persistent demand that Buganda's representatives to the National Assembly be nominated by the Lukiko acting as an electoral college provided the Lukiko was directly elected. The two parties had no quarrel over the form of government. They took the view that *"For forms of government, let fools contest that which is best administered is best"*. (Alexander Pope from The Essay on Man). I must add that the formula for indirect elections for the twenty-one representatives from Buganda obtained tactical support of the 'honest broker', thereby sealing the fate of the Democratic Party. Incensed by the dire consequences of such arrangement, Benedicto Kiwanuka, in his characteristic way, tried to stage a walk out from the conference. It was too late.

With those outstanding problems out of the way, the country went to the polls on April 25, 1962. The Uganda Peoples Congress won 37 seats to DP's 24. That was not a clear majority. Hence, the decisive and vital role played by the previously arranged political pact that came to be known as the UPC/KY alliance. It is needless to go into the merits and demerits of the alliance at this stage. What is pertinent is that the alliance made it possible for Ugandans to go forward and achieve independence as one united country with pledges to make Uganda prosperous and the happiest spot on earth.

Chapter Five

Uganda Attains Independence

"The price of liberty is perpetual vigilance." (Stephen Leacock).

It was the night of October 9th 1962 when Uganda became an independent sovereign state. There was rejoicing all over the country. African traditional drums were pounding in all the villages. There were bonfires around homesteads. Rural towns were beautifully decorated, some with electric lights of all colours. In KAMPALA, the capital city, streets and public places were throbbing with people who had travelled from all over the country to witness the big day. Uganda was poised to cast off the cloack of British imperialism.

Somewhere in Kololo, one of the many hills of Kampala, crowds of people from all walks of life milled around the airstrip to witness the hauling down of the Union Jack and the hoisting of the Uganda flag. The colours of the new Uganda flag had been a subject of controversial but lively debate in the National Assembly only a few months previously. The ceremony was an external symbolic act of the transfer of power. Uganda had become of age and taken its rightful place in the community of nations.

But the actual handing over of the instruments of independence had to wait for another twelve hours until the formal opening of the FIRST PARLIAMENT OF UGANDA. The ceremony took place at ELEVEN O'CLOCK in the forenoon of WEDNESDAY THE TENTH DAY OF

OCTOBER IN THE YEAR OF OUR LORD ONE THOUSAND NINE HUNDRED AND SIXTY TWO.

The solemn ceremony was held in the National Assembly Chamber at Parliament House. Parliament house is located right in the Civic Centre of the country's capital. His Royal Highness, the Duke of Kent, a cousin of Queen Elizabeth 11, performed the ceremony amidst pomp and splendour befitting such a momentous occasion. Among the distinguished guests present were Hereditary rulers, namely, Rukirabasaija Agutamba, the Omukama of Bunyoro-Kitara, Sir Tito Winyi IV, Rubambansi, Omugabe of Ankole, Sir Charles Godfrey Gasyonga, Sabasajja, the Kabaka of Buganda, Sir Edward Mutesa 11, Rukirabasaija, the Omukama of Toro, Sir George Rukidi 11, and Isebantu, the Kyabazinga of Busoga, Sir William Wilberforce Nadiope. From the non-kingdom districts came secretary-generals to represent their local governments. The Chief Justice and the judges of the High Court were in attendance in their brightly coloured robes as if to remind Ugandans that the newly gained freedom would be defended and safeguarded by the courts.

It was indeed a great occasion in the history of political development in Uganda. For the parliamentarians and those who believe in an orderly transfer of power it was not only a moving and impressive ceremony but a source of gratification and inspiration. On the other hand, the day was the end of the road for the ultra-conservatives who throughout the struggle for independence sought, with a certain amount of justification, to have political power handed over to a non-representative quasi-Federal Assembly rather than to a strong central legislature composed of elected representatives. All in all it was a day dedicated to an institution that was designed and destined to play a central and vital role in the public affairs of the young nation moulded from peoples of highly varied backgrounds and cultures. Political and opinion leaders throughout the country recognised the multitude of the challenges that lay ahead. They were all mindful of what needed to be done to make the new state of Uganda a reality. The task ahead was outlined by the governor, Sir Walter Coutts, K.C.M.G; M. B. E. on November 21, 1961. In his address to the Legislative Council he enjoined the leaders to ensure:

* That the aims and objectives of the new constitution are understood and supported by the great
majority of the people;
* That the processes of elections are conducted fairly and with the sense of responsibility and awareness of the basic issues of all sides;

* That the essential tenets of law and order are respected and supported by all citizens and that the human rights enshrined in the constitution are upheld;
* That the civil service is properly manned, efficiently organised and loyal in all its actions;
* That the country's economic potential does not go unrealised for lack of understanding on the part of human beings involved or for lack of adequate effort on their part.[15]

Those were some of the prerequisite to the building of a contented, stable and united Uganda. I shall return to these aims and objectives at a later stage with particular emphasis on the processes of elections, respect and observance of the rule of law and the country's record on human rights in the post-independence period.

Similar sentiments were echoed by His Royal Highness, the Duke of Kent G. C. V. D. when he opened the First Session of the First Parliament of Uganda, Wednesday, October 10th 1962. The letters patent empowering him to do so is appended.

His Royal Highness, the Duke of Kent, then delivered the speech from the throne as follows: -

Mr Speaker and Honourable Members of the National Assembly:

"I have it in command from her Majesty the Queen to read the following speech on Her Majesty's behalf.

Mr Speaker, Honourable Members: my government in Uganda is now the Government of an independent sovereign state, with complete constitutional responsibility for the conduct of its affairs in every field. I am confident that my ministers will be guided, in the solemn discharge of their principles of democracy, which are so firmly enshrined in the Uganda Constitution.

In its conduct of external affairs, my Uganda government will seek to promote international order and understanding. My government has already, since the attainment of independence, sought membership of the United Nations, and it undertakes to adhere faithfully to the charter. My government is proud of Uganda's membership of the Commonwealth of Nations, and looks forward to the development of increasingly friendly relations with the other commonwealth countries. It will seek to live in harmony with all freedom loving peoples of the world. It will do its utmost to establish fraternal connections with neighbouring countries and other

15   Hansard, Forty First Meeting (1961) p.1818

governments in Africa. The strengthening of the close links, which already bind the East African countries, will be a constant aim of my ministers.

My government's first objective, in carrying out its responsibilities within Uganda will be to foster the spirit of tolerance and good will between all the peoples of Uganda. It will aim to stimulate confidence in the future of Uganda as a united country, bound together in common nationhood. It will at the same time pay due heed to the traditional beliefs and customs of the diverse people of Uganda. It will respect the individual rights of the common man. It will, under the constitution, recognise the special status and dignity of the Hereditary Rulers and of the Kingdoms of the Constitutional Heads of the Districts.

My government, in its plans for economic and social development, will have as its first objective the raising of the living of standards of the people. My government is determined vigorously to pursue its development programme, in spite of financial stringency, which it faces at the present time. My government in Uganda wishes to express its sincere gratitude for the economic and financial help, which it is receiving from my government in the United Kingdom and from other countries.

My government will continue the orderly development of the social services. Uganda is particularly proud of its progress in the field of education, and my government is determined to continue the expansion of its educational system in all its aspects.

My government recognises the need to improve upon the workings of the regional Administrations-the Kingdom Governments, the District Administrations and the Urban authorities. It is determined to continue to foster their efficiency and viability.

My government pledges itself to respect the independence of the judiciary and the equality of all persons before the law.

My government desires to ensure that the country has an efficient, impartial and contented civil service. The policy of Ugandanisation will continue as fast as possible, having regard to the necessity to maintain adequate standards. At the same time, my government will continue to employ those expatriate officers whose services the country needs.

Finally, the ministers of my Uganda government solemnly and sincerely pledge themselves to serve the people of Uganda with faith and fortitude and to combat unceasingly the evils of hunger, disease, poverty and ignorance.

In reply, the Prime Minister, the Hon A.M. Obote spoke as follows:

Mr Speaker, on behalf of all the honourable members of this Assembly, I beg leave to offer to Her Majesty the Queen this address of thanks for the gracious speech which has marked the opening of this First Session of the Parliament of independent Uganda.

I am confident that I speak for every member of this House when I express the very great pleasure that it gives us to have their Royal Highnesses the Duke and Duchess of Kent with us today on Her Majesty's behalf.

We are a new nation with a comparatively short parliamentary history, but we are conscious that our parliamentary institution does not stand in isolation, but forms part of a system, great network of democratically elected legislatures that stretches throughout the commonwealth and to many parts of the world. The commonwealth institutions are built upon a traditional British parliamentary system, which has been established over many centuries. We are proud to be part of this tradition, for we in Uganda place great importance on traditional institutions. Throughout the great changes that have taken place during the protectorate era, we have retained and moulded our traditions to play an important part in modern Uganda. Inevitably there have been difficulties in doing this, but we believe that we have succeeded and that these traditions will form a firm foundation upon which our newly independent State can advance.

In Her Majesty's most gracious speech, she has spoken of her government's plans for the future. To fulfil all our aims, we shall require the concerted efforts of every Ugandan. If we work together we can achieve our highest ambitions. We can create a nation of which we can all justifiably be proud. But if we think first of groups and factions we shall not succeed. I am confident that we, the people of Uganda, have the wisdom and maturity to understand this, and to work together as one people in developing our new nation.

Mr Speaker, Uganda is a country blessed with rich soil, an excellent climate, and great natural beauty. The people of Uganda are, by their work and enterprise, developing extensive agricultural industries. It is our mission to continue to develop the country's natural resources, and to build up related industries. We intend not only to be a free nation but a prosperous nation. To achieve this, we shall need help both in terms of money and skilled staff. Already we are receiving generous aid from the United Kingdom and other sources. We are very grateful for this, and hope that it may continue. With the help of friendly nations, we shall go forward as a strong, freedom loving independent state.

Mr. Speaker, we are determined to succeed in the trials that lie ahead. I know we shall succeed.

Sir, it may please Her Most Gracious majesty to accept the sincere thanks of this House for the gracious speech with which the First Session of our Parliament has been opened. That marked the end of the ceremony. Ugandans were left on their own. What happened thereafter is the subject of this book.

Appendix 1

Letters Patent

The Speaker, Sir John Bowes Griffin read the Letters patent empowering His Royal Highness to open the Parliament.

Elizabeth the second by the Grace of God of the United Kingdom of Great Britain and Northern Ireland and of Our other Realms and Territories Queen Head Of The Common Wealth Defender of The Faith To Our Trusty And Well Beloved Sir Walter Fleming Coutts Knight Commander of Our Most Distinguished Order of Saint Michael and Saint George Member of our Most Excellent Order of The British Empire Governor- General and Commander in Chief of Uganda and Sir John Bowes Griffin Knight one of our Counsel learned in the law of our Bahamas Islands Speaker of the National Assembly of our Parliament of Uganda and to our trusty and well beloved the Members of the said National Assembly and our People Of Uganda Greeting: Whereas by the Uganda Independence Act 1962, provision is made for the attainment by Uganda of fully responsible status within the Commonwealth And whereas in pursuance of the provisions of the constitution set out in the Uganda (independence) Order in Council 1962, Our Parliament of Uganda has been summoned to meet for certain arduous and urgent affairs concerning the government thereof And whereas we are desirous of marking the importance of the opening of the first meeting of the said Parliament and of showing our special interest in welfare of Our Loyal Subjects therein and for as much as for certain causes, We cannot conveniently be present threat in our Royal Person.

Now Know Ye that We are trusting in the discretion fidelity and care of Our most dear and entirely beloved cousin Edward George Nicholas Paul Patrick, Duke Of Kent Knight Grand Cross Of Our Royal Victorian Order Do Give And grant by the tenor of these Present unto the Duke of Kent full power in Our name to hold Our Parliament of Uganda and to open and declare and cause to be opened and declared the causes of holding the same and to do everything which for Us and by Us shall be therein to be done Willing that the Duke of Kent shall hereby convey our said Parliament and people Our Royal message of goodwill and Our assurance of Our earnest prayer to the blessing of Almighty God on the new Constitution of Uganda and for the continued prosperity and happiness of all.

Appendix 2

Members of Government of Uganda

The Government of Uganda as constituted by the Prime Minister Hon. A. M. Obote on the May 1st 1962.

MEMBERS OF THE CABINET

THE PRIME MINISTER (also holding the portfolio of Internal Affairs)

(The Hon. A. M. Obote, M. P.)

THE MINISTER OF JUSTICE

(The Hon. G. S. K. Ibingira)

THE MINISTER OF FINANCE

(The Hon. A. K. Sempa, M. P; M. L. A.)

THE MINISTER OF ECONOMIC AFFAIRS

(The Hon. J. T. Simpson, C. B. E; M. P; M. L. A.)

THE MINISTER OF REGIONAL ADMINISTRATIONS

(The Hon. C. J. Obwangor, M. P.)

THE MINISTER OF ANIMAL INDUSTRY, GAME AND FISHERIES

(The Hon. J. K. Babiiha M. P.)

THE MINISTER OF HEALTH

(The Hon. Dr. E. B. S. Lumu, M. P.)

THE MINISTER OF AGRICULTURE AND COPERATIVES

(The Hon. M. M. Ngobi, M. P. M. L. A.)

THE MINISTER OF WORKS AND LABOUR

(The Hon. F. K. Onama M. P.)

THE MINISTER OF MINERALS AND WATER RESOURCES
(The Hon. J. W. Lwamafa, M. P.)
THE MINISTER OF EDUCATION
(The Hon. Dr. J. S. L. Zake M. P.)
THE MINISTER WITHOUT PORTIFOLIO
(Prime Ministers Office)
(The Hon. B. K. Kirya, M. P; M. L. A.)
THE MINISTER OF COMMUNITY DEVELOPMENT
(The Hon. L. Kalule -Setala, M. P.)
THE MINISTER OF STATE
(The Prime Ministers Office)
(The Hon. G. B.K Magezi, M. P.)
THE MINISTER OF INFORMATION, BROADCASTING AND
TOURISM
(The A. A. Nekyon, M. P.)
THE MINISTER WITHOUT PORTIFOLIO
(Ministry of Economic Affairs)
(The Hon. Mayanja- Nkangi, M. P.)
THE DEPUTY MINISTER OF INTERNAL AFFAIRS
(The Hon. N. M. Patel, M. P.)

PARLIAMENTARY SECRETARIES
OFFICE OF THE PRIME MINISTER
(The Hon. A. A. Ojera)
MINISTRY OF FINANCE
(The Hon. S. N. Odaka)
MINISTRY OF ECONOMIC AFFAIRS
(The Hon. S. K. Nkutu)
MINISTRY OF REGIONAL ADMINISTRATION
(The Hon. C. B. Katiti)
MINISTRY OF ANIMAL INDUSTRY, GAME AND
FISHERIES
(The Hon. K. K. K. Karegyesa)
MINISTRY OF HEALTH
(The Hon. J. N. K. Wakholi)
MINISTRY OF AGRICULTURE AND CO-OPERATIVES
(The Hon. L. Lubowa)
MINISTRY OF WORKS AND LABOUR
(The Hon. S. K. Masembe- Kabali)

MINISTRY OF EDUCATION
(The Hon W. Kalema)
MINISTRY OF COMMUNITY DEVELOPMENT
(The Hon. Mrs. F. Lubega)
MINISTRY OF INFORMATION BROADCASTING AND TOURISM
(The Hon P. Munyagwa- Nsibirwa)

ALPHABETICAL LIST OF MEMBERS OF NATIONAL ASSEMBLY

The Hon. H. E. Abdala- Anyuru, Lango West
The Hon. J. O. Anyoti Teso West
The Hon. S. Arain, Specially Elected Member
The Hon. J. K. Babiha, Specially Elected Member
The Hon. Z. R. Babukika, Kigezi South
The Hon. E. Babumba, Masaka North West
The Hon. A. K. Balinda, Toro Central
The Hon. D.B. Barisagara, Kigezi West
The Hon. B. K. Bataringaya, North West
The Hon. A. G. Bazanyamaso, Kigezi- South- West
The Hon. G. L. Binaisa, The Attorney General
The Hon. E. N. Bisamunyu, Kigezi East
The Hon. E. B. Bwambale, Toro South
The Hon. B. Byanyima, Ankole North East
The Hon. Y. Chemongenes, Sebei and Bugisu North
The Hon. M. L. Choudry, Karamoja North
The Hon. J. Ekaju, Teso North
The Hon. G. S. K. Ibingira, Ankole West
The Hon. S. E. Isiagi, Teso, South East
The Hon. S. B. Jaffer, Kampala West
The Hon. W. W. Kalema, Kome
The Hon. L. Kalule Settala, Mengo South East
The Hon. A. J. R. Kangaho, Ankole South West
The Hon. F. J. I. Kangwamu, Ankole South East
The Hon. K. K. K. Karegyesa, Kigezi North
The Hon. A. Kasakya, Bukedi South Central
The Hon. P. Kasujja, Mubende South and Gomba
The Hon. C. B. Katiti, Ankole Central
The Hon. P. Kiggundu, Specially Elected Member

The Hon. D. M. Kimaswa, Bugisu South East

The Hon. B. K. Kirya, Bukedi North Central

The Hon. Y. M. Kirya, Busoga East

The Hon. A. Kisekka, Mengo South

The Hon. J. W. Kiwanuka, Mubende North

The Hon. M. H. Kuhikya, Bunyoro East

The Hon. S. W. Kulubya, C. B. E; Specially Elected Member

The Hon. G. A. Kassim Lakha, Specially Elected Member

The Hon. E. Y. Lakidi, Acholi North

The Hon. A. A. Latim, Acholi North West

The Hon. A. Y. Lobidra, West Nile and Madi North West

The Hon. D. D. Lobunei, Karamoja South

The Hon. J. P. Loruk, Karamoja Central

The Hon. H. M. Luande, Kampala East

The Hon. Mrs. F. A. Lubega, Singo North West

The Hon. L. Lubowa, Bulemezi South

The Hon. B. Lukyamuzi, Masaka North

The Hon. E. B. S. Lumu, Kyadondo North

The Hon. J. W. Lwamafa, Kigezi South East

The Hon. C. J. M. Magara, Bunyoro South West

The Hon. G. B. K. Magezi, Specially Elected Member

The Hon. S. K. Masembe- Kabali, Mityana

The Hon. J. S. Mayanja Nkangi, Masaka East

The Hon. M. N. Mehta, Specially Elected Member

The Hon. T. C. K. Mudhungu, Busoga North East

The Hon. S. G. Muduku, Bugisu North West

The Hon. F. X, B, Mugeni, Bukedi South

The Hon. E. M. K. Mulira, Mengo North

The Hon. Z. Munaba, Busoga Central

The Hon. P. Munyagwa Nsibirwa, Bugerere

The Hon. Y. M. Musitwa, Mengo Central

The Hon. P. Muwanga, Specially Elected Member

The Hon. A. A. Nekyon, Lango South East

The Hon. K. M. Ngirisi, Toro North West

The Hon. M. M. Ngobi, Busoga South

The Hon. S. K. Nkutu, Busoga South East

The Hon. A. N. Nume, Busoga North West

The Hon. J. H. Obonyo, Acholi South East

The Hon. A. M. Obote, Lango North East

The Hon. C. J. Obwangor, Teso East
The Hon. J. S. M. Ochola, Bukedi South West
The Hon. G. O. B. Oda, West Nile and Madi West
The Hon. S. N. Odaka, Jinja North
The Hon. A. A. Ojera, Acholi South West
The Hon. J. M. Okae Lango Central
The Hon M. A. Okelo, West Nile and Madi Central
The Hon. S. K. Okurut, Teso South
The Hon. M. O. K. Omadi, Bukedi North
The Hon. D. A. Patel, Kampala South
The Hon. M. K. Patel, Jinja South
The Hon. N. M. Patel, Mbale
The Hon. V. K. Rwamwaro, Toro East
The Hon. F. G. Sembeguya, Specially Elected Member
The Hon. A. K. Sempa, Sezibwa West
The Hon. P. N. Serumaga, Masaka South West
The Hon. J. T. Simpson, C. B. E. Kyagwe North West
The Hon. I. Sebunya, Mengo South West
The Hon. S. W. Uringi, West Nile and Madi South
The Hon. Mrs. Sugra H. A. Visram, Kibuga
The Hon. J. N. K. Wakholi, Bugisu South West
The Hon. J. S. L. Zake, Masaka Central

LEADER OF GOVERNMENT BUSINESS
The Hon. C. J. Obwangor, M. P.

GOVERNMENT CHIEF WHIP
The Hon. A. A. Ojera, M. P.

LEADER OF THE OPPOSITION:
The Hon. B. K. Bataringaya, M. P.
The Hon. F. J. I. Kangwamu took his seat on 10th December 1962 following a bye- election in Ankole South East Constituency.

PRINCIPAL OFFICERS AND OFFICIALS OF THE NATIONAL ASSEMBLY
THE SPEAKER   The Hon Sir John Griffin, Q. C.
THE DEPUTY SPEAKER... ... ...The Hon S. W. Kulubya, C. B. E; M. P.

THE CLERK OF THE NATIONAL ASSEMBLY...Mr. Phillip Pullicino

THE FIRST CLERK ASSISTANT... ... ... Mr. B. N. I. Barungi

THE GENERAL DUTIES ASSISTANT ...Mrs. N. A. Patel

THE SEARGENT AT ARMS ...... Mr. I. Rwothonga

THE ASSISTANT SEARGENT AT ARMS...Mr. A. K. Kato

THE ACCOUNTS ASSISTANT ... Mr. C. Mbalire

THE ACCOUNTS CLERK... Mr. W. Munyani

THE EDITOR OH HANSARD.... . Mrs. M. Campbell

PALANTYPE OPERATORS.... . Miss M. Mclean

Mr. N. Venkateswaran

Chapter Six

Evolution Of Political Institutions

In any given society, there can be no coherent social life unless the social relationships that bind the people together are to a certain extent orderly, institutionalised and predictable. The only alternative to such arrangement is anarchy or chaos. Hence, there is a need to look for 'norms' and 'rules' that sustain a given social order. In this chapter an attempt is made to trace the process of the small beginnings of some of Uganda's political institutions, mainly the executive and administrative structures, the legislature and political parties. It is only through such institutions that authority can be exercised under a shared system of values. The major underlying issues that came to shape the evolution of political institutions in Uganda were: land problems in Buganda, the question of a closer East African Union, then ethnicity and religious rivalry. These were matters that aroused political consciousness and awareness in such a way as to mould present-day Uganda. It is important to highlight their impact on society.

Land Problem in Buganda

Land, especially in Buganda, played a great part in arousing political consciousness. After the First World War the administration took certain measures to reactivate economic activities. A development commission was established to put the economy on a peacetime footing. Initially, the Europeans were the principal growers of cotton on large cotton plantations. The Africans provided labour on the plantations. That state of affairs did not last long. The administration soon started encouraging Africans to grow cotton to raise money for poll tax. In the process the Africans started using the surplus cash to buy manufactured goods imported from overseas. This also proved to be a source of revenue for the administration because imported goods were taxed. The growing of cash crops by the Africans on their individual smallholdings did not please plantation owners. It depleted the available labour force. Another factor cropped up. The administration prohibited the sale of land to non-Africans. The move was bitterly contested by the Europeans and the Asians but to no avail. Because of the acute shortage of labour and land the big cotton plantations collapsed shortly before the slump of 1920. However, the growing of cotton was resumed after the slump. A Cotton Control Board was formed consisting of government officials, Ginners' Association, Chamber of Commerce and the Middlemen Association. Meanwhile, the growing of coffee had taken root in Bugisu and two pulping stations were established. Here again, African farmers were in the lead. E.B Jarvis, acting Governor, acknowledged the contribution the Africans were making to the economy when he addressed the Annual Conference of the Uganda Planters Association. He said, "The more I turn over the matter in my mind, the more convinced I become that Uganda's future lies in the cultivation of the soil and the growing of the crops by the natives under scientific supervision by the Agricultural Department and the purchasing and marketing of these crops by Europeans." [16] This was a pregnant statement that raised a number of issues, namely, land ownership, the enjoyment of the fruits of labour and the marketing of the crops grown by Africans. Land was the immediate major issue. The 1900 Agreement between the Kabaka of Buganda and the British Government created a landed gentry in Buganda.

The 1900 Buganda Agreement had a far-reaching impact on the social and political life of the people in the Kingdom of Buganda. Social status, privilege and power were bestowed on the Christians who were loyal to the British. A total of 3700 persons were allocated land. The three regents were Apollo Kaggwa (Prime Minister), Zakaria Kisingiri (Kangawo saza chief) and Stanislus Mugwanya who was also prime minister representing the Catholic faithful, each received tracks of land ranging from 45 to 60 square miles. Others obtained between eight and twelve square miles while the majority of the allotees got one to two square miles each. The bulk of the population were left out, particularly the Bataka at the lower level known as *siga* level in the Kiganda tradition. The Bataka performed certain duties for the Kabaka. They were the traditional link between the Kabaka and

16   Professor K. Ingham: *History of East Africa*, Longmans, 1962, p331.

the ordinary people – clanspersons who in the new set-up were reduced to the status of tenants under the new landlords. In the political field the Bataka ceased to sit in the Lukiko, which the British turned into a formal Council, composed of chiefs only.

Prior to the 1900 Agreement, the Kabaka exercised executive power over the kingdom. Because Daudi Chwa was a minor when he ascended the throne, a regency consisting of chiefs was established. For all intents and purposes, power moved from the Kabaka to the chiefs who at the same time controlled the Lukiko. Twenty years later a few educated Baganda realised that the Agreement of 1900 had revolutionised the ownership of land. The majority of the population had been deprived of their customary rights. In the past sub-clan leaders held land in trust for members of their clans, especially burial places. Now the new landed gentry were blocking access to those burial places.

Before the introduction of the cash economy chiefs were allowed to collect 'busulu' (ground rent) or 'nvujo' (commodity rent) from the inhabitants living under their jurisdiction. That changed. The 'busulu/nvujo' were replaced by wages in cash. Since the chiefs were at the same time landlords the colonial administration allowed them to collect rent from the people who lived on or cultivated the land. More often than not the chiefs continued with the 'busulu' and 'envujo' practice. As a matter of fact demands were made for exorbitant tributes. The 'Bataka', the clan leaders began to complain very bitterly. They petitioned the Kabaka who prior to the Agreement of 1900 exercised control over land.

Attempts for redress were rejected by the Lukiko, which was dominated by the chiefs. It then dawned on the ordinary people that the Kabaka had actually lost his power to the chiefs who had consolidated their position during the long period of regency. The Protectorate government showed no sympathy to the 'Bataka'. The least they could do was to pass the 'busulu' and 'envujo' law which gave protection to the tenant in the enjoyment of the fruits of his labour while at the same time guaranteed a reasonable rent to the landlord. It is doubtful whether even such minor relief could have been granted during Apollo Kagwa's administration. He had thwarted earlier moves of reform or compromise. Elsewhere in the Protectorate attempts were made to introduce certificates of occupancy particularly in the Western Province. The experiment was not effective. In Busoga the chiefs were simply not interested in the new system of land tenure. The eighty-five square miles set aside for allocation to chiefs were withdrawn. So, it was only in Buganda that land caused great conflict between the chiefs and the ordinary people. The situation created by the new land tenure is described by Roland Oliver thus: "Johnson's land settlement in Buganda caused initially a period of great confusion while claimants were scrambling for their shares peasant cultivators moved about in despair seeking a place in which to settle." [17] This is the historical background that gave rise to the riots of 1945 and 1949. We shall see the comparative great changes that took place in the composition of the Legislative Council between 1945-1950 when the number of African representatives was increased to eight by the end of that period. This in a way increased the impetus for the Africans to participate in the public affairs of their country and the few politically enlightened men thought it was high time to form a national political party to organise and to mobilise the masses to fight for independence.

The Question of closer East African Union

The events of 1940-5 and particularly the aftermath of the Second World War had a direct political impact on Uganda. The other issue that attracted public debate and sparked off a wave of nationalism in Uganda was the possibility of a federation or closer union of the East African Territories. This was a matter of great importance that provoked a heated public debate among Africans between the First World War and the Second World War. The issue aroused among the Africans for the first time the feeling of togetherness and a sense of common destiny. Professor Kenneth Ingham recalls: "If circumstances shaped a rarity of approaches to the political and administrative problems of the three East African territories there was one political factor which disturbed them all. That was the idea of closer union, no less disturbing because it was never clearly defined. But closer union had another claim to attention besides the opposition it aroused in East Africa. For unlike almost every other policy proposal before the Second World War it originated entirely in Britain, and drew no strength from East Africa itself"[18]

Immediately after the First World War the white settlers in Kenya demanded self- government. The British government favoured or preferred gradual progress towards that goal. A public statement to that effect was made in His Majesty's Government White Paper of 1923. The White Paper declared inter alia: "African interests in Kenya must be paramount but that there would be no drastic reversal of the conditions under which

17   Roland Oliver: * *Sir Harry Johnston and the Scramble for Africa Chatto and Windus*, London 1959 (P329).

18   *History of East Africa* (Longmans 1962), p.310.

Europeans and Indians had established in the territory." So, when rumours of closer union reached Kenya, the white settlers condemned the proposal and considered it to be diversionary because it would undermine their own plan for self-government. Lord Delamore their leader declared that he felt strongly that for the next few years Kenya should stand alone, if it was to realise its ideals of civilisation and progress as a self-governing colony and had digested the problems of that country first. In Tanganyika, the Kilimanjaro Planters Association was apprehensive and feared domination by Kenya. The Europeans in Uganda also took the same view. It was not until 1924 that the Africans in Uganda came out in opposition to the idea. A commission under the Honourable W. Ormsby-Gore was sent to East Africa "to consider and report on the measurers to be taken to accelerate the general economic development of British East Africa and on means of securing closer co-ordination of policy over transport, cotton growing and medical and agricultural matters"[19] On this occasion, the Kabaka and the Lukiko of Buganda, pointing out that the terms of the Agreement of 1900 would be adversely affected by the new arrangement, submitted a memorandum. All in all, the Commission reported that the countries of East Africa were not in favour of closer union. However, the Commissioner made a proposal that the three governors should meet at certain intervals to discuss and review problems of national interest. Meanwhile, the Kenya settlers changed their attitude towards the proposal. Delamore changed tactics. He wanted to consolidate the white settlers position in the legislative council by securing a majority and then press for an East African Federation. He met with settlers' representatives from Central Africa to interest them in the Scheme. Nothing came of the two meetings. Tanganyika was still opposed to the proposal.

The idea of closer union lingered on. In 1927 a White Paper was issued detailing recommendations of a sub-committee. The sub-committee recommended the termination of separate individual developments hitherto enjoyed by the three territories. To implement the recommendations, a new commission headed by Sir Hilton Young was appointed in December 1927 to find out whether federation was desirable. The people of East Africa were still opposed to the idea. Eventually the matter was referred to a joint committee of both Houses of Parliament appointed in 1930. Uganda sent a delegation to London in 1931. The delegation consisted of saza chiefs: Kosiya K. Labwoni, (Bunyoro) Yekoniya Zirabamuzale (Busoga),

19   I.E Huxley, *White Man's Country*, Macmilan, London 1953 Vol. II (P83-84).

Serwano Kulubya and Samson Bazongere (Buganda). The three delegates were accompanied by C. L. Burton, one of the district officers in Uganda at the time who in his opening remarks during the deliberations told the Joint Committee: "My Lords, the Uganda Protectorate contains within its boundaries tribes at every stage of development, from primitive savagery to a condition approximating to an elementary Western civilisation."[20] This was after thirty years of British colonial rule and shows the type of arrogance Ugandans were subjected to for another thirty years.

Tanganyika also sent a delegation of Africans. Apparently, the committee members were impressed by the arguments put forward by the African delegations who argued that since they wanted to develop their own institutions they would rather remain under the control of the Secretary of State, instead of answering to a Commissioner based in Nairobi. The whites in Kenya and Tanganyika reacted violently when the British Government showed sympathy to the views expressed by the African representatives. The truth is that the people of Uganda particularly in the Kingdoms were weary of any changes that might have given the white settlers in Kenya power to control the Africans in Uganda, as was the case in Kenya. There was also genuine fear that any such change might increase immigration of non-Africans to Uganda. For once, the Hereditary Rulers acted in concert with the people to oppose what was conceived to be a direct threat of white domination. The East African Standard proclaimed "Where in history has a civilization been established in primitive and backward regions in which the whole or principal aim is to safeguard the interests of savagery and ignore the paramount pressure of progress and enlightenment":[21] Nonetheless, the Joint Select Committee recommended against closer union of a political or constitutional character. Instead, the Governors' Conference was strengthened and given an increasing role in the co-ordination of policies in the three territories. The Governor's Conference did not have a constitutional framework. It took decisions without prior consultations with or consent of the territorial legislatures. All the same, the conference served a useful purpose. To rectify the situation, it was proposed to establish an East African High Commission, consisting of the three governors, an executive organisation and a Central Legislature. That was the beginning of the East African Common Services culminating in the East African Community of the post-independence period. The

20   *Joint Committee on Closer Union in East Africa Vol. 11 Minutes of Evidence:* (Her Majesty's Stationery Office, London 1931).
21   *East African Standard* June 23,1930.

Community collapsed in 1977 when ordinary communication among the East African top political leadership succumbed due to the politics of personality. Efforts are underway to revive the Community. Unfortunately, the political leadership refuses to learn from history. For the community to succeed we must build it from the grassroots and not from the top that is often subjected to the vagaries of the volatile African politics. All structures of the future community need to be institutionalised.

Ethnicity and Religious Rivalry

I have already mentioned the seeds of religious discord that were planted by the colonialists at the beginning of their rule in Uganda. Moslems, Catholics and Protestants fought one another during the religious wars of 1880-90. The wars did not end until the colonial power agents came to the aid of one of the religious factions. The practical effect of that policy was the marginalization of the Catholics and Moslems. Protestantism became for all intents and purposes the official religion of the Protectorate. Non-protestants suffered discrimination in almost all fields of civic life. Appointment of chiefs throughout the country was based on religion. In Buganda and in the other kingdoms top positions of chiefs were reserved for Protestants. The result was that the majority of chiefs throughout the breath and length of the country were men who professed to be Protestant faithfuls. Awards of bursaries and scholarships by the various district and kingdom administrations followed a similar pattern. Placement in general employment was no exception. The Catholics were relegated to minor and inconsequential positions. The Moslems came off the worst of all because for a long time they had no access to education. In the early times education was provided in parochial schools that were controlled by the Christian missionaries. In the circumstances the 1955 constitutional reforms that introduced an element of the principle of representation in both the District Councils, including the Buganda Lukiko, and the Legislative Council at the Central Government level, ignited every conceivable latent political force in the entire social spectrum. It was obvious that the days of colonialism were numbered. The pertinent and burning question was who would step in the shoes of the colonial masters? Buganda and the other kingdoms had a hidden feeling that the colonial power would restore the pre-colonial status quo by merely updating the agreements between the kingdoms and the Imperial power. Political groups thought otherwise. They contended that times had changed. The Protectorate would emerge from colonialism as a nation state comprising of all the nationalities that made up Uganda. That was the catch. Henceforth, all political developments pointed in that direction. To the Catholics in Buganda, the reforms were a challenge. They were convinced that the moment had come for them to regain lost political ground and influence. According to available statistics they formed the majority in Buganda, and figured that they could mobilise sufficient votes to control the Buganda Lukiko (Parliament). Their major player was Matayo Mugwanya, Omulamuzi(Chief Judge) at Mengo who had his eye on the office of the Katikiro (Prime Minister) hitherto a Protestant preserve. In the true spirit of Protestant chauvinism, the Mengo establishment closed ranks to ensure the preservation of the existing Protestant hegemony. When the time came, Matayo Mugwanya, the Catholic candidate for the post, was defeated. The mathematical calculations did not tally with the political realities on the ground. In order to keep the spirit of revival alive he tried to secure a seat in the Lukiko. He was denied the chance and lost. That infuriated the catholic elite in Buganda who turned for support to their fellow Catholic sisters and brothers in the rest of the country. They posed the question, "What further evidence do you need to take action?" They immediately launched a nationwide political party. The Democratic Party was born in 1956. Having been born out of frustration, the main objective of the party was to seek redress for the injustices meted out to catholics during the colonial era. It was a tall order. Matayo Mugwanya became the first President General of the party. Those were the circumstances under which the party came into being. Because of the frustration experienced by Catholics throughout the country at the hands of Protestants , the DP found ready help from the Catholic church structures at all levels. Surprisingly, the new party got assistance and encouragement from unexpected quarters, including the colonial administration. At that point in time the DP became handy for the colonial regime. The Uganda National Congress, which by 1956 had been in existence for four years, was proving to be a problem child for the administration. Because socialism was in vogue especially among the oppressed peoples of the world, the UNC embraced socialism. It was UNC's advocacy of socialism that set the party and the colonial administration on a collision course. It is important to note that those were the days of the cold war. The British and the Americans took it upon themselves to guard and save the African continent from that monster called communism. One wonders whether they ever took the trouble to find out that, apart from a handful of African intellectuals, the vast majority of the Africans had no idea whatsoever about communism.

Whatever capacity they could muster was exhausted by the mere effort to earn a living. They had neither the energy nor the leisure to understand the complexities of communism. In their campaign and resolve to fight communism the Western powers found a capable and willing partner in the Catholic church not only in Uganda but throughout the world. In the event, the DP was well-disposed to join the crusade and became a pliable tool in the campaign against the UNC and later the UPC - successor to the UNC. The ethnic and religious conflict scenario that has bedevilled this country is aptly described by David Apter in the preface to the second edition of his book, *The Political Kingdom of Uganda* (Princeton Press, 1967). He says: "Prior to independence, a series of concessions had been made, giving Buganda federal status, thereby securing the autonomy laid down in the 1900 Agreement and granting similar status to other kingdom states. The constituency parties of the UPC were a growing force, offsetting the religious, clan, ethnic and constitutional rivalries which had for so long been the basis of Uganda's political life."

Political Parties

> *"A Political Party is a body of men united for promoting by their joint endeavour the national interests upon some particular principle in which they are agreed."* (Edmund Burke).

Nobody will deny the existence of political parties in Uganda. On he contrary, there were over half a dozen political parties towards the close of 1950s. But the challenge was to establish parties on a national basis in the face of interest groups and divisions in the country. It is often argued that the attainment of independence came rather late considering the fact that Uganda was a protectorate and not a colony. The assumption, here, is that for 'a protectorate', the colonial power could at any time quit if asked by the inhabitants to do so. In practice that was not the case. Uganda became a British possession through all sorts of means, including the use of the maxim gun. In theory the colonial power concluded separate agreements with the Hereditary Rulers of Buganda, Toro, Ankole and other subdued paramount chiefs. The pertinent question is: were the hereditary rulers in a position to bargain or negotiate with the powerful invading colonialists?

In any case the famous agreements did not stipulate the duration of the British stay in those kingdoms. In the final analysis there was no material difference between the two terms. Ugandans had to fight for their freedom. We have seen that everywhere the invaders went they were met with resistance in one form or another. After the establishment of the

Uganda Protectorate, law and order became the major preoccupation of the colonial administration otherwise economic exploitation would have been impossible. Because of their experience elsewhere the British chose to use the local people to maintain law and order. The hereditary Rulers in the Kingdoms and Paramount Chiefs elsewhere were deployed for the purpose. Administrative units in most cases were based on nationalities. A hierarchy of chiefs was established throughout the country and was superimposed by a cadre of colonial administrators to superintend the work of the chiefs. The indirect rule system created power centres at the nationality levels each of which dealt directly with the Governor as Chief Executive of the Protectorate. The upshot of it all was that the inhabitants of this country continued for a long time to think in terms of their own separate nationalities. Consequently, the growth of political parties at a National level was exceedingly slow.

Some people will argue that lack of national consciousness in the early days of colonisation was due to the fact that the inhabitants of what came to be called Uganda were drawn from a variety of nationalities who speak different languages and hold different religious beliefs. That would be a great fallacy since a nation in a political sense need not be a union of people of one descent nor of one language group or belong to one religion. The older nations of Europe namely the United Kingdom, France and Switzerland are examples in point not to mention the United States of America. As Leacock Stephen puts it, "The real bond of union, the underlying bedrock in which the structure of a nation rests, is the willingness to unite the unity of hearts that takes the opportunity that is given"[22] With hindsight it is conceded that the imposition of British rule over us could have afforded an opportunity to forge and project a sense of nationhood if we had collectively put up and sustained resistance against the invaders. That of course was not possible. Uganda at that time was a mere geographical expression. There was no co-ordination among the various principalities. Besides, the principalities or nationalities were not strong enough to resist the superior power of the maxim gun employed by Captain Lugard and his henchmen such as Semei Kakungulu.

In many ways, the Uganda National Congress founded in 1952 could be described as the lineal descendant of the peasant grievances and the Bataka organisational efforts. By that time, the British dictum of divide and rule had taken too deep a root to be uprooted effectively within a short space of hardly ten years before Uganda attained independence. Even after the formation of the first ever national political party a great deal of

22   *Elements of Political Science* (1906).

precious time was spent on stressing the differences between ethnic groups and working out safeguards for hereditary rulers in the different kingdoms. There was also the question of Asian minorities. Such issues were, to a certain extent, diversionary. In the end as will become evident national unity was wrecked on the rock of pseudo-federal structures ostensibly to protect and safeguard the positions Hereditary Rulers. The UNC as it was popularly known was formed by a few highly dedicated persons whose sole aim was to tear down nationality barriers that hitherto had stood in the way of political unity and progress. The founder members of the party were Messrs. Ignatius Musazi, Abubakar Mayanja, Joseph W. Kiwanuka and Dr. Barnabas Nyamayarwo Kununka. They were later joined by men like Milton Obote from Lango, Otema Alimadi from Acholi, George Kamba from Bukedi and many others. These men spearheaded in earnest the battle for freedom and Uganda owes them a great deal for their rare pioneering spirit in the political field which at that time was considered highly dangerous because of the attitude of the colonial masters towards political activists. Besides the hostile colonial attitude the party's political base, Buganda, was not always sympathetic to the aims and objectives of the UNC. Indeed, very often there was a clash of interest between the two.

The broader leadership of the UNC was drawn from the petty bourgeois intelligentsia. The membership covered farmers and small businessmen. There was another group of members, the professionals who had voluntarily retired from the civil service in protest against the oppressive terms and conditions of service meted out to African professionals not to mention the high handedness of the white colonial officials.

By 1955 the Uganda National Congress could boast of a total membership of about 50,000 mainly from the Western Province, Buganda, Bukedi, Acholi, Lango and Teso. The last three districts were leaders in cotton production. The UNC had all the ingredients of a truly national party fully committed to the struggle for independence and the realisation of economic well being of the indigenous Ugandans. The party will go down in our history of political development as a political organisation that rekindled the torch for the freedom struggle initiated by Omukama Kabalega and Kabaka Mwanga and other elder freedom fighters. My first contact with the UNC was in 1957. I was a student at the University of Delhi, India. Dr B. N. Kununka was then Secretary General of the party. He was in Delhi to attend the annual conference of the Commonwealth Parliamentary Association. Uganda was an affiliated member of the

Association. Dr B. N. Kununka was representing the Legislative Council. The Uganda Students Association (India) of which I was Secretary General considered his presence in Delhi a golden opportunity for putting their views across to a high-ranking official of the UNC and an active member of LEGCO.

The Uganda Students Association was concerned about the slow advancement of Uganda to independence. The association and the party shared a great deal of common ground. The students expressed reservation about the party's lack of proper organisation, the absence of a comprehensive manifesto and the party's inability to speak out boldly on issues that tended to derail Uganda's march to independence as a strong united country. One interesting incident took place during Dr. Kununka's stay in Delhi. The delegates to the conference were staying at Ashok Hotel – a very prestigious hotel at the time. One evening Dr. Kununka flanked by Uganda Students met with a delegate from Southern Rhodesia, (now Zimbabwe). The delegate was no other than Ian Smith. He was having a hot argument with some students from Northern and Southern Rhodesia. We joined the group. The burning question of the moment was whether or not the Central African Federation ought to be maintained. The African students were totally against the Federation because they argued it was designed to perpetuate white rule in Central Africa. Ian Smith could not fathom the students' audacity to oppose the colonial regime policy in Central Africa. Smith was visibly upset by the students' uncompromising attitude. He lost his temper and did not mince his words about what he thought of the Africans as a whole. He declared in no uncertain terms that there would never be majority rule in Central and Southern Africa. I know for sure that the students from Central Africa did not take Smith's utterances lying down. They definitely did more than attend lectures at the university during their stay in India. Men like Munakayumwa Sepalu of Zambia and William Chokani from Malawi took up the challenge. I did not hear of Ian Smith until November 1965 when he declared Unilateral Independence for Southern Rhodesia (Zimbabwe). He lived long enough to witness a government led by the black majority. Such is the dynamics of politics.

Talking of visits reminds me of another personality who paid an official visit to New Delhi shortly after the political reforms of 1958 that introduced a ministerial type of government. The visitor was no other than 'Minister' Yusufu Lule who was in charge of Social Services and Trade Development. His Permanent Secretary, a Mr R. F. Roper, accompanied him. At the time the author was Secretary General of the Uganda Students in India. It was his responsibility to make arrangements through the All India Council for Cultural Relations for the visiting party to meet the Uganda students. Because the spirit of Africanism was so strong among African students, representatives of students from other African countries were invited to the meeting, which took place at Janpath Hotel in the centre of New Delhi. The purpose of the meeting was to review the political situation in Uganda, in particular and imperialism in Africa in general. The students felt uneasy to hold such a discussion with the visiting minister in the presence of an imperialist agent. The students' sentiments were duly conveyed to the Minister prior to the scheduled meeting. But the message made no impression on him. Consequently, on the appointed day he turned up with his Permanent Secretary. The welcoming team reminded him of the students' stand and told him in no uncertain terms that if he insisted on Mr. Roper's presence, there would be no meeting. That precipitated a minor confrontation. In the end the meeting took place without R. F. Roper.

At the end of the day the students felt a sense of self-fulfilment. They had exposed the Minister to the ideals of pan-Africanism, made a political statement that the ultimate objective for Uganda was independence, and pronounced the patronising attitude of the colonial administrators unacceptable. We moved on with our lives for a better day. The better day came when President Kwame Nkrumah of Ghana paid a state visit to India. His visit made a great impact on millions of Indians when Jawaharlal Nehru, their idol, received in person the visiting President and hosted him at a public government reception to which we were all invited. Thereafter, the Indian population began to take greater interest in the African students' community and could no longer afford to ignore the momentous political developments that were unfolding on the continent.

A lot of unkind words have been said about UNC. Some people attribute its ultimate collapse to the 'inability to attract the more forward looking and best educated in Buganda'. Relations between the party and Mengo establishment were initially tolerable and in fact became cordial during the period of the Kabaka's deportation. That is why in the 1955 democratisation process of the Lukiko and the Legislative Council, the Buganda representatives to LEGCO were all UNC members. The strain began in 1958 when as Professor Dan M. Mudoola puts it "The response of the Buganda ruling groups to the rise of political parties and proposed democratisation of the Legislative Council was one of fear for Buganda's status as they perceived it. A democratically elected Legislative Council dominated by political parties would imperil Buganda's Kitibwa."[23] The Central issue was Buganda's status and the position of the Kabaka. Buganda's hostility was not directed to the UNC per se. It was a general attitude to political parties as an institution. What is relevant here is that Buganda's attitude towards political parties deprived the UNC of a vital political base as UNC leadership at the time was mainly from Buganda. But there were other forces at work. It may be recalled that the first President of the party, Ignatius Musazi had already been in the forefront of politics in Buganda. He played a leading role in organising African Farmers Union. Musazi was assisted by two prominent members of the British Labour Party, Fenner Brockway and John Stonehouse who were renown for their leftist political views. Fenner Brockway (later Lord) was totally against colonialism in all its shades. The two Britons were also involved in advising Musazi in the establishment of the Uganda National Congress. Stonehouse spent almost a year with Musazi and his team. Such an association in the days of the cold war was unacceptable to the western world. To add insult to injury, right from its inception the UNC made contact with the Eastern Block. They secured scholarships for the needy Ugandans to study in the Iron Curtain countries. The party developed strong ties with Ghana, Yugoslavia and China as time went on. These contacts could only invite the wrath of the western powers. The party was perceived as communist-oriented. The gap widened between the colonial administration and UNC when the latter opened an office in Cairo, and joined the Afro-Asian Solidarity Committee, which had its headquarters in Cairo. John Kalekezi, youthful and energetic, was in charge of the Cairo office. Kale, as he was intimately known, died in a plane crash on his way to Moscow in the company of other Afro-Asians Solidarity Committee delegates to the famous trial of Gary Powers, the pilot of the U2 United States plane that was shot down in the Soviet Union on May Day 1960. Mahmood Mamdani aptly summarises the cause of the party's disintegration: "Opposition to militant nationalism took two forms, the first was orgnised outside the UNC, in direct opposition to its militant orientation and was spear-headed by the Democratic Party (DP), marching under the banner of Catholicism and anti-communism. Secondly opposition to militant nationalism grew within the UNC itself."[24]

23   *Religion Ethnicity and Politics in Uganda* (Fountain Publishers Kampala, Uganda) p22.
24   *Imperialism and Fascism in Uganda* , (Heinmann Education Books {EA} Ltd) p21.

Be that as it may, the biggest force for the undoing of the UNC was the British colonial regime, which went out of its way to do everything possible to ensure total collapse of the party. There was no way UNC could survive the colonial onslaught. It is, therefore, safe to assert that what wrecked the Uganda National Congress was a combination of forces including personal ambitions of the leaders that led to their reluctance to hold regular party elections to bring about change in the leadership from time to time. That was an unfortunate development that was to haunt all future political parties in Uganda for a long time. It is now certain that the absence of well-organised political parties on a sound basis greatly contributed to the failure of the parliamentary democracy experiment in Uganda.

The Uganda Peoples Congress dominated Uganda's political scene for over thirty years. To be able to grasp the complexes of the peculiar history of Uganda's political development one needs to examine the central role-played by the Congress. I will attempt to evaluate its performance, assess its successes and take note of its trials and tribulations. In carrying out this appraisal I have not lost sight of the fact that the UPC was an offshoot of the Uganda National Congress, which spear-headed the political struggle for independence. The UPC inherited the main characteristics of the parent party. For instance, it assumed the UNC historical mission of moulding a united 'Nation State' out of the various nationalities that made up the British Protectorate. The UPC adopted a pragmatic approach to the country's problems but retained the political dynamism of UNC. The new party articulated and expounded its aims and objectives in clearer terms and then set out an appropriate strategy to achieve the objectives. Top on the agenda was the struggle for independence. Thereafter the main thrust of the aims and objectives was to

- Maintain and defend the territorial integrity and sovereignty of Uganda,
- Build a peaceful, stable prosperous and egalitarian society by fighting rentlessly against poverty, ignorance and disease;
- And in the external sphere the party pledged total commitment to the maintenance of cordial relations with the immediate neighbouring countries and the pursuit of positive non-alignment policy in international affairs.

At the outset the UPC had an edge over all other parties. Before the 1961 elections, the UPC boasted of a number of outstanding personalities in the legislative council who had gained valuable experience in parliamentary procedures and techniques. Because daily proceedings of the Legislative

Council were broadcast countrywide many of these members had acquired the stature of national figures. After the 1961 elections these members formed an inner core of the opposition. The opposition had a field day. Much of the credit for their performance in the Legislative Council goes to a small group of dedicated gentlemen. The author happened to be a member of the Legislative Council staff at the time. He was able to observe the effort and contribution made by each one of them. The group consisted of J.K. Babiiha, G.S. Ibingira, J.B.T. Kakonge, K.K. Karyegyesa, C.B. Katiiti, B.K. Kirya, J.W. Lwamafa, G.B.K. Magezi, W.W.K. Nadiope, A.A. Nekyon, M.M. Ngobi and C.B. Obwangor. A.M. Obote led the group.

The Democratic Party won the 1961 elections. DP obtained 43 seats to UPC's 35. However UPC did extremely well because it collected a total of 488,334 votes against DP's 407,461. Why was that? This was due to the fact that the elections were not free and fair in Buganda. The Mengo establishment, as explained elsewhere, did not favour the holding of elections before the status of Buganda and the position of the Kabaka were spelt out. So, Buganda mounted a campaign against the elections. Through intimidation and acts of violence the majority of eligible voters were not able to register. In certain instances even those who managed to register were not able to cast their vote due to intimidation. Out of the estimated 700,000 potential voters only 35,000 people had the courage to register. Most of those who braved the odds were DP supporters. Accordingly, DP was able to secure twenty-one seats from Buganda. It is arguable whether DP would have been able to win so many seats in an environment free from political intimidation and violence. As a matter of fact, the Mengo establishment went beyond the boycott of registration and elections. Towards the end of 1960 the Buganda Lukiko (Parliament) passed a resolution to the effect that Buganda should go it alone by declaring unilateral independence on January 1961. The British administration ignored the purported resolution and the threat. January 1, 1961 went off without any untoward incident. Appropriate security measures were taken. Indeed, it was on the eve of the new year (1961), while taking an evening ride to Mengo that I sighted for the first time a soldier of the Kings' African Rifles by the roadside as part of the military deployment in Kampala to highlight the resolve by the administration that peace would be maintained at any cost. A little more than five years later a similar situation occured but took a different turn altogether when the Buganda Lukiko passed a resolution ordering the Government of Uganda to quit Buganda land. There was confrontation between the Kabaka's Government and the Uganda Central Government, as will be explained later.

Faced with the intransigence of the Mengo establishment coupled with the western kingdoms' reluctance to embrace a unitary form of government for Uganda, UPC had to take stock of the prevailing political situation. Realism dawned on the leadership of the party. The party decided to adopt a strategy of flexibility and understanding. But the notion that UPC leadership went on bended knees to seek a political alliance with Buganda for purposes of gaining power is based on unresearched work. The fact is that Mengo, nay, Twekobe (palace) took the initiative.

It must be remembered that the population at large wanted to be free. They wanted to cast away the colonial yoke. So, the attainment of independence became paramount. The general consensus was that minor differences among conflicting groups would be ironed out once the main objective (independence) was achieved. The first attempt to tackle these differences was the talks held in September 1961 at the First Pre-Independence London Constitutional Conference. That was the time that fortune started to smile on the Uganda Peoples Congress. However, I must hasten to add that the 'fortune smile' theory does not portray a proper assessment of the delicate and complicated political situation at hand. To be sure, the UPC-KY alliance was tricky. It needed a lot of effort and a great deal of soul-searching. The move was full of risks. The UPC leadership needed extraordinary courage to go for it. There was the estrangement of the Youth and the radical nationalists who saw the alliance as a retrogressive step calculated to entrench the ultra-tradionalists or conservatives who were deadly opposed to political party politics. There was the alienation of the Bunyoro Kingdom and her sympathisers who looked at the alliance with suspicion and that in the face of the alliance, the UPC stand on the question of the lost counties would favour Buganda. There was also fear that the incumbent Prime Minister could turn the tables at the polls proposed to be held in the month of April 1962 to precede independence. Despite all the misgivings the UPC leadership held the view that the formation of an alliance was the way forward. It was worth the risks. There were also positive signs that the alliance would, at least in the short run, yield good results. For instance, Buganda came on board and joined the march towards independence along with other political organisations.

The Second London Conference accepted and adopted the major recommendations of the Munster Commission on Relationships. What is relevant here is the provision that Buganda's representatives to the National Assembly would be nominated by the great Lukiko provided the Lukiko was directly elected. That in itself sealed the outcome of the April general elections. The UPC backed by the Kabaka Yekka was able to form a government led by Apollo Milton Obote. The main theme of this work is devoted to the party's attempt to implement two of its main objectives, namely, the maintenance of the territorial integrity and sovereignty of Uganda and the building of a peaceful, stable, prosperous and egalitarian society. The achievement of the latter objective proved, as we shall see, elusive.

Chapter Seven

The Lost Counties And
The Constitutional Process

"He censures God who quarrels with the imperfections of Men",
(Edmund Burke).

It would be appropriate at this juncture to have a closer look at the Lost Counties issue that turned out to be a thorn in the country's body politic during the first two years of independence.

A comprehensive study of the Lost Counties issue lays bare the full impact of British imperialism in Uganda, exposes the intricacies of the working of the doctrine of divide and rule and shows human nature at its worst- the vindictive nature of man. The Lost Counties dispute arose out of the unjust wars waged by the British colonialists against the people of Bunyoro Kitara. We have seen that two hundred years ago Bunyoro Kitara was a great kingdom, extending far beyond her present boundaries, especially to the South and East. Kabalega Chwa II put up a great resistance to preserve his kingdom. As a result of that resistance, counties of Bunyoro Kitara were annexed to Buganda and came to be known as "The Lost Counties". This formed a long-standing dispute between the kingdoms of Bunyoro and Buganda. The dispute arose from the dismemberment of Bunyoro-Kitara by transferring to Buganda in 1900 the counties of Buyaga, Bugangaizi, Buhekula, Buruli, Bulemezi and Bugerere. That was a penalty inflicted upon Omukama Kabalega and the people of Bunyoro-Kitara for having waged a war against British invaders.

It was at the same time a reward to collaborationist Buganda for "services rendered". To strangle and weaken the kingdom further, Capt Lugard installed fugitive Kasagama, son of dissident Prince Nyaika, as King of Toro. The dismemberment of the kingdom of Bunyoro Kitara was purely a vindictive and ill-conceived punitive action on the part of the colonial administration. The evidence from tradition is that by the beginning of the 19th century, Buganda was advancing her position from what had originally been a relatively small principality upon the North Western shore of the lake. Not until the subsequent alliance with the British in the reign of Mwanga (Mutesa's successor), did Buganda make substantial gains of territory at Bunyoro's expense.

We learn from oral history and from history books that the kingdom of Toro was pure and simple a creation of the British Empire builders. "Lugard, accordingly, left Buddu in June 1891, taking with him a young prince who had settled as a fugitive in Buganda and was the rightful heir to the chieftainship of Toro which had been overrun some years previously by Kabalega of Bunyoro"[25] As a matter of fact Kabalega had only reasserted the authority of Bunyoro-Kitara in his earlier campaign to reclaim and consolidate the ancient kingdom.

The Lost Counties understandably generated a great deal of animosity between Buganda and Bunyoro. The issue has always been a constant reminder of the violent overthrow of Kabalega and the deprivation imposed upon the people of Bunyoro. We recall with sadness that by 1899, after the war of resistance, Bunyoro Kitara was in a very poor shape. It was utterly devastated, its inhabitants ravaged by famine and disease and its administration in total chaos. To paraphrase Audrey Richards, "The degradation of the ancient kingdom was almost complete". That was exactly what the empire builders set out to achieve. But the worst was yet to come, for the 1900 Agreement between Britain and Buganda transferred Bunyoro's richest counties of Bugangaizi, Buhekula, Buyaga, Bugerere and Buruli to Buganda in recognition of the services rendered to the British administration by the likes of Kakungulu during the bloody and protracted war with Bunyoro Kitara. In terms of human resources, the territorial transfer represented forty percent of Bunyoro Kitara's population. Is it any wonder that today's population of Bunyoro is so negligible? Following the devastation caused by the war, thousands of Banyoro migrated to distant areas, some as far as Mombasa. The exodus further diminished the population. To add insult to injury, Bunyoro was for all intents and

25   Thomas and Scott "Uganda" p.31.

purposes, treated as a conquered territory for the first thirty years of British colonial rule. The people were subjected to mental and psychological torture. The British and their cronies made it their business to run down the Banyoro as a community.

The British administrators went out of their way to depict Banyoro as lazy and undisciplined people. Worse still, they made sure that Bunyoro was denied educational facilities. Missionary- run schools in Bunyoro were deliberately starved of funds. That propaganda notwithstanding, the Banyoro, as a community, stood firm. They have over the years shown that they are intelligent, energetic, industrious and tenacious. Despite the fact that by the time of independence there was not a single secondary school in the whole of Bunyoro, the kingdom was able to get a fairly good number of well-educated people who managed to get access to educational institutions outside the kingdom. It is ironic that the Banyoro community was the first to produce a woman university graduate in the person of Sarah Ntiro Nyendwoha. At the inaugural lecture held at the International Conference Centre, Kampala, in December 2001 to commemorate her achievements, she was described as 'the African girl child from Bunyoro-Kitara who dared swim against the tide and became the woman of many firsts'. She excelled in mathematics at Kings College Budo and was admitted to Makerere College, now Makerere University Kampla. After a spell of teaching, she was admitted to Oxford University where she graduated with a Bachelor of Arts Honours Degree in History. The author first met her when she was a member of the Legislative Council. She was one of the first two African women members of the Council. Unlike many backbenchers of her time, Sarah Nyendwoha often made quality contribution to the proceedings and deliberations of the Council. Who knows, the Banyoro could have produced many more Nyendwohas if they had been given the opportunity The bottom line was denial of opportunities. Given equal opportunities the Banyoro are capable of competing favourably with anybody and completely acquit themselves of the insults and false claims that have been heaped on their community by detractors.

To prove their tenacity, the Banyoro living in the Lost Counties formed the Bunyoro Mubende Committee in 1921 whose sole purpose was to spear-head the struggle for the return of the lost counties to Bunyoro Kitara. The formation of the Committee and the campaign mounted by the Bunyoro Kingdom local government went to prove that the very idea of transferring part of Bunyoro to Buganda in the hope that the people living in those counties would sever their cultural ties with Bunyoro was an act of criminal folly. Far from demoralising the Banyoro, it helped keep alive the old fighting spirit. Several delegations were sent to London to present the Lost Counties issue to the British government, petitions were submitted to the Queen of England and to the Privy Council as well. With the help of the best British lawyers Bunyoro managed to build a formidable case.

Endowed with their traditional fighting spirit and convinced of their just cause, the Banyoro were able to keep the question of the Lost Counties alive up to the time of the pre-independence London conference. Suddenly, the British who for years had been non-committal, acknowledged the magnitude of the problem. There was no way the British government could have continued to sweep the problem under the carpet. Doing so would have been a disaster for Uganda. The best the British government did was to place the problem in cold storage for two years with the full knowledge that by that time they would have relinquished their responsibilities in Uganda. That decision and action did not reflect what admirers of the British way of life call "the British sense of fair play". Indeed, this is an opportune moment to pay tribute to two gallant British junior officers who had enough courage to express great sympathy with the Banyoro over the territorial loss of Bugangaizi, Buyaga, Buhekula, Rugonjo, Buruli and Bugerere.

The two exceptional British administrators saw the dismemberment of the kingdom of Bunyoro Kitara as a case of great injustice. J.R. Posthethwaite was one of such administrators who were sympathetic to the cause of Bunyoro and made every effort to persuade the Banyoro to come to terms with what had befallen them by forgetting the past and bracing themselves for the task ahead of rebuilding their country. The other administrator was Pulteny who was detailed and sent to transfer the counties to Buganda. He chose to resign. Posthethwaite arrived in Uganda in the year 1909. He began his career as Assistant treasurer in Entebbe and served as assistant District Commissioner in various districts, including Teso, Acholi and Busoga. It was during his tenure of office as District Commissioner in Bunyoro - August 27,1927 to July 22,1928, when he won the hearts of the Banyoro. His wide experience gathered in the course of his service in different parts of Uganda made him realise and appreciate the grievances of the Banyoro and their aspirations.

He was convinced that the actions of Kabalega and his people in opposing foreign control hardly merited the consequences that followed it. This is what he wrote in his report about the lost counties, " The inclusion of this area in the Buganda kingdom is considered by many to have been one of the greatest blunders we committed in the past, its correction if it is to be corrected could only come with the consent of the Kabaka and the native government of Buganda... we might justifiably *insist on the Banyoro as subjects of the Kabaka being given at least a greater share in the governing of Bunyoro portion of the Buganda kingdom,* in case it seemed impossible to make up for the loss to the unfortunate Banyoro of what was in fact their holy of holies and the real centre of the ancient kingdom. (Emphasis is mine) It was only an accident after all that at the time of the Buganda agreement, the Baganda were temporarily in ascendancy. *Incidentally, the caves of the rocky hills near Kakumiro had been a standing place of the Banyoro from which as far as I know, the Baganda had never successfully dislodged them, while in Buyaga lie the graves of Banyoro Bakama, where every creature, hill, rock and blade of grass cries aloud to those interested that they are Banyoro and can never be anything else.*"[26] At the time of his departure from Bunyoro, Tito Gafabusa Winyi II, the Omukama of Bunyoro wrote him a letter in which he conveyed on behalf of the kingdom, his appreciation and the Banyoro's gratitude for supporting their cause. The Omukama told the administrator that he would always cherish the thought that it was Posthethwaite who improved his country by building good roads, fine camps brought about increased food production and introduced the growing of cotton and tobacco as cash crops. It was during the term of office of J.R. Posthethwaite and others like him that a great deal was initiated to improve the lot of the Banyoro by creating a conducive political environment and treating them like human beings and giving due respect to the Omukama and his chiefs.

Never before had Bunyoro seen such developmental activities- new roads were constructed, agricultural production increased by leaps and bounds, Masindi port was developed, a sisal estate was established near the new port and saw milling in Budongo Forest started in earnest. To crown it all, Bunyoro Kitara ceased to be treated as a conquered territory by signing the 1933 agreement between the kingdom of Bunyoro and the British colonial administration. This period can be described as the hey-day of Bunyoro since the fall of Omukama Kabalega. No similar economic development of that magnitude and social impact have been experienced again in the last fifty years or so.

There is need to critically look at the ramifications of the lost counties' issue in its wider perspective. In the first instance what happened in the

26   Dunbar, *A History of Bunyoro Kitara* (Oxford University Press 1965) p102.

counties of Buyaga, Bugangaizi, Buhekula, Buruli, Rugonjo and Bugerere smacks of Christian ethics. I have elsewhere in the preceding pages outlined the role played by Christian missionaries in the "pacification of Buganda in particular and what came to be known as Uganda in general".

In the spirit of Christianity as understood today, it is inconceivable that such inhuman treatment was meted out to the inhabitants of the lost counties in the full glare of the Christian missionaries and that nowhere in their volumes of literature on their zeal to convert pagans do we come across any protest by the influential missionaries over the plight of the inhabitants living in those counties. Both the Roman Catholic Church and the successors of the Church Missionary Society owe the Banyoro an explanation for their muted behaviour. It is not too late to clear the air. There is no doubt that the people in the lost counties were subjected to the worst type of colonialism ever experienced in Uganda. They were prohibited to use their mother tongue in the courts of law, schools and public places. Most young women had to adopt non-Kinyoro names, otherwise they would not be eligible for bursaries let alone secure employment in the Local administration. Now that the existence of oil in commercial quantities has been confirmed, the government of Uganda has an obligation to set in train plans to rectify imbalances in development which the people of 'the lost counties' have suffered for so long. That should include necessary reforms in favour of the inhabitants.

What infuriated the Banyoro was the knowledge that if some reactionary elements had not assisted the British, Kabalega and his people would have been saved from the ravages of that war. We now know that men like Apollo Kaggwa, who later became Katikiro of Buganda and General Kakungulu were used by the British to fight against anybody who opposed British rule. They were deployed in Bunyoro to fight Kabalega's army. The same people fought against Kabaka Mwanga who after realising that the ultimate objective of the British was to subjugate his people and bring his kingdom under British rule, decided to defend his kingdom. Sadly, by the time he declared war on the imperialists, his subjects were already divided on religious grounds. Day after day, he had to contend with uprisings fomented by religious leaders- Catholics, Protestants and Moslems. In the end, he joined hands with his brother Omukama Kabalega in an attempt to stave off the British menace. The two kings, Uganda's premier freedom fighters were defeated, captured, humiliated and sent into exile. Uganda's historians and scholars have neglected or omitted telling the people of this country at large the true story about these two great men.

In this perspective, the issue of the lost counties question ceases to be a purely tribal issue, it forms a corner stone of British colonial policy in Uganda. It is clear that the partition and dismemberment of Bunyoro was a carefully caltulated plan by the British administrators to sow what they regarded as a permanent seed of discord between Buganda and Bunyoro. It was a device that fitted well in their doctrine of divide and rule. They succeeded in keeping the future generations of Bunyoro and Buganda and their respective rulers in constant conflict. Previous co-operation and goodwill between the two nationalities ceased. Professors, travellers and sundry have written to confirm the British story that Buganda and Bunyoro were natural enemies. There was no such a thing. Rivalry, there was because the two communities were neighbours. Instances of cooperation between the two kingdoms abound in history. Oral history tells us the two communities maintained contact. There was even an exchange of presents occasionally between their reigning monarchs. It is said that Mutesa I sent a contingent of men to help Kabalega's rival during the short war of succession to the throne. Kalema was installed as king with the help of Kabalega. The British colonialists and the Christian Missionaries were greatly incensed by Kabalega's assistance to Kabaka Kalema because the latter had chosen to become a Moslem and was supported by the Arab traders.

Throughout the colonial era, young boys and girls were taught at school to regard Kabalega and Mwanga as outlaws and savages. The two are often described as men who killed for pleasure and brought untold misery to the people. At the same time, suspected traitors are depicted as heroes and men of great courage and intelligence. It is high time Ugandan historians exposed these lies.

Chapter Eight

The Origin And Growth Of Uganda's Legislature

Origins are usually obscure. The parliament of Uganda was no exception. The National Assembly did not simply spring up at the time of independence. It was one of those vital institutions that evolved and developed over a long period of time. A historical account of its development gives yet another insight into the people's struggle for freedom and independence. On the whole the political development in Uganda followed the British norm of the the colonial pattern with one exception. While in a country like Ghana the indigenous people in that country were associated with their legislature right from its inception, in Uganda the colonial administrators closed their eyes and the Ugandan Africans were shut out of the legislative council.

For the first twenty-five years of its existence the Africans were not members of the council. The essence was not to develop a system based on the principle of representation. Basic tenets of imperialism did not permit that. The criterion was economic consideration. Uganda's economy did not perform as well as was expected. The output of rubber and cocoa plantations fell below expectation. Matters were not helped by high transportation costs – a problem we continue to reckon with to the present day. Capital for development became scarce after the First World War, following the great depression. So the colonial regime had to rely on industrial and commercial interest groups to mobilise capital for meaningful development. There were two main interest groups involved in commerce and industry – the Europeans and Asians. Europeans were planters and exporters, while Asians engaged in commerce and money lending. These interest groups demanded a voice in the country's political affairs. The governor found it expedient to set up a body of advisors who he could consult from time to time. That is how the legislative council came into being in 1920. However, it did not meet until the following year. The Europeans and Asians monopolised both the executive council and the legislative council to the total exclusion of the Africans for the next twenty-five years. That was done, notwithstanding the fact that after the depression of the 1920s, emphasis shifted from large plantations, owned and managed by Europeans, to African agriculture. Cotton and later coffee became the leading export crops. At the beginning Africans needed something more than persuasion. The growing of the two crops, especially cotton, became an entirely 'administrative' issue. Cotton had to be grown at any cost and the chiefs saw to that. However, with the growth of import trade a lot of manufactured goods started coming into the country. As the demand for imported goods grew, the people felt the need to grow more cotton and coffee out of their own free will to raise sufficient funds to acquire the imported manufactured goods. The political cost of excluding the Africans from the legislative council for so long has been heavy for this country. We were denied a political forum that would have brought together people from all corners of the country to discuss issues of common interest at a national level. Our early participation in such a forum would have enabled us to cultivate a sense of national consciousness and to forge unity of purpose. Our participation in the legislative council at an early date would also have changed the role the chiefs played in the political life of the country. As a matter of fact, the first batch of Africans to sit in the council in 1945-49 was not representative. They were top senior chiefs from Buganda, the Western Kingdoms, Busoga and Eastern and Northern regions.

Before the legislative council was set up, the commissioner or the governor made laws in accordance with the 1902, order-in-council. In making the laws, the governor was assisted by his senior civil service advisors. It was not, as we have seen, until 1920 that a Legislative Council was established by the order in council of the June 29. The main characteristic of the council was that it was not representative. Its original membership was made up of four government officials and two unofficial members, all of whom were Europeans. The Governor presided over the proceedings of the council. This practice continued until the end of 1957.

Thereafter, the speaker presided at all meetings of the Legislative Council. The first speaker was Sir John Griffin, a retired Chief Justice of the High Court of Uganda who had considerable experience, not only in legal affairs, but also in administrative matters. He made a name for himself in 1954 when he ruled that the deportation order served on the Kabaka of Buganda in 1953 was made under a wrong article of the 1900 Buganda Agreement. Unlike the governor the speaker had neither an original vote nor a casting vote. Meetings of the council were held in the High Court at Entebbe until 1945 when Kampala became the new venue. But it was not until 1960 when the legislative council finally acquired its own premises, which were inaugurated by Iain Macleod who was then Secretary of State for the colonies.

In the process of colonising Uganda Britain brought a large number of Asian immigrants, mostly of Indian and Pakistan descent. The majority of them were hired to work on the Uganda-Kenya railway between 1896 and 1901. After completion of the railway, the Asians were allowed to settle both in Kenya and in Uganda. A lot more followed with the result that they soon dominated trade, commerce ,and even the Civil service. Little did the colonialists know that they were creating not only a racial problem but a social problem too. By the early twenties there was a sizeable community of Asians in Kampala.

It was in the light of this that the governor invited them to nominate one of their number to represent them in the Legislative Council. Strange as it may sound, the offer was turned down on the grounds that a single representative would not be adequate. However, in 1926 the first Asian member was sworn in and in 1933 a second Asian member took his seat. That brought the membership to 6 official and 4 unofficial. It may be recalled that a similar argument was made shortly before independence when Britain advocated special safeguards for Asians. The indigenous Ugandans were at that time politically awake and would have none of that claim. Besides, the young Asian generation advocated for integration as indicated later.

In fact, the campaign by the Asians for minority safeguards and adequate representation generated a great deal of heat and was partly responsible for the boycott of Asian-owned shops and goods by the Africans in the late 1950s. The upshot of it all, was that, although the Asians dropped the claim, seeds of discord had been sown and mistrust between the two communities continued even after independence. During the struggle for independence members of the Asian community were accused of sitting on the fence. That kind of behaviour did not endear them to the African freedom fighters. However, what is of great significance is that the colonialists had the impudence of inviting a handful of Asians to nominate a representative to the Legislative Council while ignoring the existence of the Africans who by far outnumbered the whites and the Asians put together. Somebody had the audacity to say that it was the job of the official members of the Legislative Council to safeguard the interests of the Africans who were not even consulted before the Legislative Council was put in place. Never mind Buganda's reaction to the establishment of the Legislative Council in the person of Sir Apolo Kagwa. Apolo Kagwa's opposition arose out of his own interpretation of the 1900 Agreement. It had nothing to do with the future of Uganda as a whole. The exclusion of the Africans from the Legislative Council was a settled colonial policy. It was not until after the great events of the Second World War, which shook the world in general and the British Empire in particular, that three Africans were nominated to the Legislative Council. As indicated above, the nominees were already part of the colonial establishment – the chiefs who were active partners in British colonialism. For the sake of clarity the nominees were: the Katikiro (Prime Minister) of Buganda nominated by the Kabaka of Buganda, the second represented what was then the Western Province, and he was, in rotation, the Katikiro of the kingdoms of Ankole, Bunyoro and Toro, the third member represented the Eastern Province and he was, also in rotation, the Secretary General of the districts of Busoga, Bugisu, Bukedi and Teso. The African representative for the Northern Province took his seat four years later in 1949. That looked like a policy of separate development. The following year the number of African representatives was doubled. Thus, the colonial government was able to hoodwink the African population for sometime since their numerical strength in the Legislative Council had been "enormously' increased. But in reality, despite the increase of seats, the African took no part in the formulation of policy, not even in the day to day administration of the country. All representatives were nominated. There was one other factor that influenced political events in the 1950s. In 1938 a group of what I might call nascent politicians in Buganda began a crusade against the combined tyranny perpetrated by the British administrators and the Baganda chiefs drawn from the upcoming 'landed gentry'. The struggle revolved around the membership of the Buganda Lukiko that was totally unrepresentative. The high handedness of the chiefs supported by the colonial administration did not make matters better. There was also an explosive issue of land alienation brought about by the 1900 agreement. Most of the land was granted to chiefs. The clans were deprived of their Butaka holdings. The majority of the clansmen started a vigorous campaign to recover their Butaka holdings. At the same time the group took great exception to the naked exploitation of the African farmers (the cotton and coffee growers) by the Asian cotton ginners and coffee processors. The Africans growers felt that the Asians were cheating them. They also challenged the monopoly of Uganda Company, a British firm, over the control and sale of cotton. By early 1940s, the three prong movements had mobilised the ordinary people-peasant farmers, petty traders and workers including junior chiefs. The anti-Buganda government hostility reached its pitch in 1945 when open riots broke out. The leaders of the movements notably Ignatius K. Musazi, Spartas Mukasa and Fenekasi Musoke were detained and restricted. But they did not give up the struggle. On the contrary, the Baganda traditionalists launched the Bataka Party in 1946 that was able to establish branches at the muruka (parish) level. Two years later, Ignatius K. Musazi registered the Uganda African Farmers' Union. There was a great deal of mutual trust and co-operation between the two organisations. The Bataka directed their attack at the Mengo establishment while the Uganda African Farmers' Union concentrated its efforts on the struggle to secure fair producer prices for the African grower. The farmers made appeals to the central government. Their appeals fell on deaf ears. Once again, the leaders had no alternative but to resort to the only weapon that exploiters the world over understand – strike action.

No immediate effort was made to redress these grievances. But the message was clear and the colonial administration took note of the situation and sought to wrestle the initiative from the African militants. The African Farmers Union was proscribed under the provisions of the Co-operative Societies Ordinance of 1946. The 1952 Trade Union Ordinance forbade workers from forming general unions and decreed that separate unions be set up for each industry. The law required the unions to submit financial statements to government every year and demanded that union funds should not be used for political purposes. Since that time the trade union movement has never been strong enough to play an effective role in the politics of the country, save only when it suited politicians to serve their interests. Never again were co-operative societies of whatever description and trade union able to function as mass organisations of peasant farmers and workers. However, all was not lost. In his endeavour to secure an international market for the Uganda Association of African Farmers

Musazi made a trip to London where he met with Fenner Brockway, an outgoing labour member of parliament. Fenner Brockway and his colleagues Stonehouse and Eirene White were very sympathetic to the African cause. Out of that contact was born a long relationship between the people of Uganda and the British labour party. I.K. Musazi's contact with Fenner Brockway helped raise both his spirits and his horizon. He moved from the politics of parochialism to national politics. He got exposed to international politics. The contact led to the formation of the Uganda National Congress. The establishment of a national political party was one of the best things that ever happened in the political arena of this country. It provided a national platform that defied the well laid, water tight, political units within the confines of tribal affiliations.

The new national party opened new opportunities that would facilitate the transfer of power not only from the British foreign rulers but also from their partners, the chiefs who for long had been used as tools to oppress the population.

One might dismiss the operations of Uganda African Farmers Union and related organisations as parochial in character. In assessing the import and value of these early political activities in Buganda we must take into account that Buganda was the major centre of the country's economic activities. The cultivation of cotton and coffee was first introduced in the central region. The ginning of cotton and processing of coffee all started in Buganda. Naturally, these economic activities attracted people from all over the country. Besides, the seat of the central government was in Buganda. Many people came over to the government headquarters to seek employment. What is pertinent here is that the grievances expressed by the rioters reflected the sentiments of all farmers and workers throughout Uganda. Even the Bataka's programme of action, which was strictly directed against the iniquities of the Baganda chiefs and their style of administration, attracted attention from outside Buganda. The demand for peoples' representation in the Buganda Lukiko had similar appeal in the outlying districts of Uganda. These developments in Buganda rekindled old fears in the minds of the people of Uganda and resentment against foreign colonial rule. They had far reaching consequences. The colonial administrators realised that maintenance of law and order could no longer be enforced effectively by the security and the hierarchy of chiefs.

There is no better way to depict the mood of the times than to reproduce a text of the despatch of February 25, 1947 from the Secretary of State for colonies addressed to the governors of African territories: "I wish to emphasise the words, efficient, democratic and local. I do so not because they import any new conception into African administration, indeed these have been the aims of our policy for many years. I use these words because they seem to me to contain the kernel of the whole matter, local because the system of government must be close to the common people and their problems, efficient because it must be capable of managing the local services in a way which will help to raise the standard of living, and democratic because it must not only find a place for the growing class of educated men, but at the same time command the respect and support of the mass of the people". In a nutshell that was the British Labour Party Government colonial policy on the political, social and economic development. The emphasis was to develop an efficient and democratic local government. The term 'democratic' was later replaced by the word 'representative'. In response to the despatch Uganda's colonial governor had some explanation to make. In his view Uganda represented in herself a great degree of diversity "within this single small territory, no common sentiment of unity exists among its units. The administrative boundaries have not in all cases been drawn to conform strictly with tribal divisions and have therefore the least significance in the African mind; and in some of the districts there is a miscellany of tribal units each possessing a strong tribal consciousness and each jealous of the position of the others. Moreover, the development of indigenous political institutions in the Protectorate has been uneven, with the state of Buganda taking the lead. It is therefore a matter of prime importance to devise some unifying process which, over a period of years, will tend to produce a sense of common interest and of common purpose and later, it is hoped, of common nationality-and at the same time to encourage and not impede, the growth and development of indigenous political institutions... the Uganda government hopes to find this unifying process in a progressive development both in the executive responsibility and in their representative character, both in the system of councils with official elected members, at the levels of province, district, county, parish and village, each council acting as an electoral 'college' for the council above it. There was need to bring in greater representation of the population at large and create opportunities for them to be able to participate in the economic development of their country and enjoy the fruits of their labour". This paved the way for the establishment of District Councils under the African Local Governments Ordinance of 1948. Buganda had already been declared a corporate body ten years earlier. The political reforms were followed by great economic activity under the development plan for Uganda, which sought to increase agricultural output by twenty-five percent.

That was a formidable task. The lot fell on Sir Andrew Cohen who was then Under Secretary for African affairs in the colonial office. He was appointed Governor of Uganda. He had been intimately associated with the policy of political devolution in West Africa, which eventually led to Gold Coast (Ghana) and Nigeria advance to self-government. Sir Andrew Cohen is remembered in Uganda as an outstanding man who, despite often erratic and unimaginative policies pursued by his predecessors, he made it possible for the people of Uganda to mould out a nation of the earlier fragmented segments in water tight compartments. He took command in 1952 and the old outstanding grievances by the African population began to be addressed. Social services were expanded and large sums of money spent on schools, hospitals and roads. Co-operative societies were set up by legislation. A co-operative government department was established to oversee the co-operative movement in the country. The Africans, through growers co-operative unions, were empowered by law to acquire ginneries and coffee factories. Some political measures were also taken. The Buganda Lukiko and the district councils were reconstituted by introducing greater elected representation. On the negative side, restrictive laws were made to curb the activities of trade unions. The newly formed co-operative societies and unions were insulated from indulging in politics as organisations. He was also instrumental in the deportation of the Kabaka of Buganda.

In the meantime, a political crisis of great magnitude took place. As already indicated, limited electoral reforms were introduced in the Buganda Lukiko. The number of elected members was increased to sixty, elected through electoral colleges. The Kabaka in consultation with a Lukiko committee was to appoint three ministers. Both the governor and the Kabaka made a public announcement to the effect that "the Uganda Protectorate has been and will continue to be developed as a unitary state. The Kingdom of Buganda will continue to go forward under the government of His Highness the Kabaka and play its part in accordance with clause 3 of the 1900 Agreement, as a province and a component part of the Protectorate". The governor shortly after the statement published proposals for further changes in the composition of the legislative council. Twelve more representative members were to be appointed, bringing the total to twenty-eight, of whom fourteen were to be Africans. A few other changes were envisaged. The Mengo establishment was not entirely happy with the trend of things. Then came remarks made by the Secretary of

State for colonies, June 30, 1953, on the possibility of the East African territories coming together in a federation. The comments sparked off protests by the Mengo establishment as well as by nationalists against the central government. The government of His Highness the Kabaka repudiated the earlier reforms proposed by the central government. The old arguments advanced in the 1930's against closer union of East African territories were this time around put forward with greater vigour and an element of finality. The Buganda Lukiko passed a resolution on the issue and demanded that remedial action be taken to safeguard the future. The Lukiko strongly opposed any form of political union affecting Uganda with neighbouring territories, urged that the affairs of Buganda should revert to the foreign office, and further urged that a timetable be set up for Buganda's independence. The Kabaka in his letter of August 6, 1953, addressed to the colonial secretary highlighted the fears of the Lukiko and confirmed the demands contained in the Lukiko resolution. As if that was not enough, the hereditary rulers of Ankole, Bunyoro and Toro Kingdoms in their joint letter dated August 10, 1953, addressed to the governor, also strongly objected to the proposed federation of East Africa and expressed dissatisfaction with the guarantees given by the colonial secretary. Not to be outdone, the Uganda National Congress, for quite different reasons, endorsed the Buganda Lukiko stand. Relations between the protectorate government and the Mengo establishment reached their lowest ebb in years when the Kabaka and his government totally refused to shift their position on:

- the transfer of Buganda affairs to the foreign office
- the timetable for Buganda's independence,
- Buganda's refusal to participate in LEGCO.

The prolonged direct negotiations between the Kabaka and the governor failed to resolve the impasse. The colonial government interpreted the Kabaka's intransigence as a breach of the often quoted 1900 agreement which stipulated unqualified co-operation between the Kabaka, his people and the British government on matters of policy. Consequently, the British government withdrew recognition of His Highness Edward Mutesa II as Kabaka of Buganda. On November 30, 1953, he was deported to London. The incident set a number of things in motion. The 'nationalists' particularly the leadership of the Uganda National Congress jumped on the traditionalist bandwagon ostensibly to fight for the return of the Kabaka. There is no doubt that the nationalists had a hidden agenda as will be illustrated later. In the end Buganda proved ungovernable without the Kabaka. Fourteen years later history repeated itself after the crisis of 1966, as we shall see later. For the moment suffice to state that the crisis drastically changed Uganda's political scene. The colonial administration for the first time was put on the defensive.

The upcoming freedom fighters took full advantage of the situation. They used the deportation of the Kabaka to whip up African resentment against foreign rule. The message was simple: "Imperialists look down on everything African – his culture and his traditions. African dignity was at stake," they proclaimed. At the forefront of the campaign was the Uganda National Congress, which was founded in 1952. As stated earlier, the congress grew out of the federation of the Uganda African Farmers. The party had a large following among peasant farmers and what one would call petty traders-call it a petty bourgeois party. The UNC bore a rare characteristic. Unlike previous political groupings, which were confined to Buganda affairs, the UNC was national in outlook with branches covering the whole country. It transcended nationality barriers. That is why, right from its inception, the British colonialists were, as illustrated earlier, scared and wary of it. UNC was quick in exploiting the deportation by mobilising every social section of the population supporting the call for the immediate return of the Kabaka. They drew up a petition and sent a high-powered delegation to London to press home the peoples' demands. At the same time the UNC crystallised its demand for "Independence Now". The leaders of the party took advantage of the situation to explain to the masses that it was only by gaining self-rule that African culture and all that it stands for could be preserved and safeguarded. It was a windfall for the demagogues like Joseph Kiwanuka (intimately known as Jolly Joe) who was then a prominent member of the party. They made the best of it. For the next two years political activity was at its highest. The campaign by the congress aroused a great deal of emotion and national consciousness. The message for the need to be free reached every corner of the country. The people by and large understood the message and gave their support. In the event, major changes took place in 1955. The Hancock Committee negotiated with the Baganda elders the conditions under which the Kabaka, Edward Mutesa II, would return home from exile. The Kabakaship was to be insulated from active politics and make the Kabaka a constitutional king. The Lukiko was to appoint the Katikiro and draw up a list of persons from which the Kabaka would appoint a council of ministers. Machinery for appointing/nominating Baganda representatives to the legislative council was put in place. It is to be noted that the most important condition was that Buganda would make a solemn undertaking to participate in the legislative council in future. All forward-looking Ugandans hailed this condition. It meant marching together as one nation on the arduous road to independence. Thereafter, there was a rapid increase in the African membership of the council culminating in the introduction of a ministerial form of government in 1955.

The total membership then stood at sixty. Two distinct sides had emerged in the legislative council. One side was composed of representative members and the other was the government side. There were thirty members on each side. What is of great interest is that the Africans constituted fifty percent of the total membership. The racial standing was as follows: on the representative side there were eighteen Africans, six Europeans and six Asians. Out of the eighteen Africans, five were from Buganda, two from Busoga, two from Ankole and one from each of the following districts, Bunyoro, Toro, Kigezi, Bukedi, Bugisu, Teso, Lango, Acholi and West Nile. On the government side there were three African ministers, two parliamentary secretaries and seven backbenchers, bringing the total to twelve against eight European ministers, seven European backbenchers, one Asian minister and two Asian backbenchers. This composition was modified in 1958 when a speaker was appointed to replace the governor as a presiding officer of the council. Because the governor held two votes, one original and a casting vote, his departure from the legislative council necessitated the nomination of two additional members so that the government could maintain its majority. The two additional members happened to be Africans. It is worth noting and of great interest that the five representatives from Buganda were members of the Uganda National Congress. They came into the Legislative Council under part of the Hancock settlement, which made possible the return of the Kabaka to Uganda after the 1953 deportation crisis. There is no doubt that the 1955 political reforms marked the beginning of definitive progress on the march to responsible government. It was however far from democratisation. The members of the Legislative Council constituted an interesting assortment of men and women. In the first instance, ministers, who enjoyed and exercised extensive powers, were not responsible to anybody but the governor; secondly, those who passed as representatives were neither delegates nor the choice of the people they claimed to represent. The backbenchers were nothing but rubber stamps. "For all its law making powers, the legislative council in 1956 was basically an advisory body."[27]

27   David.E.Apter, *The Political Kingdom in Uganda* (Princeton University

It is no wonder then that the National Resistance Councils set up by Museveni's Movement during 1986 and 1989 failed to make an impact on the majority of Ugandans. For politically sensitised Ugandans the two National Resistance Councils were reminiscent of the colonial days and political organs. In the final analysis they represented retrogressive steps and were a big blow to the cause of democracy.

The 1955 political reforms were designed to develop Uganda henceforward as a unitary state with Legislative Council and the office of the governor at the centre. Greater co-operation between Buganda and the central government was expected as a necessary prerequisite if the projected political programmes were to be meaningful. The reforms were also designed to forge and promote friendly relations between the kingdom of Buganda and the rest of the country. According to the colonial secretary time was needed to absorb the effects of these and other changes. "In order to secure a period of stability for the country no major changes in the constitution should be introduced for a period of six years from 1955, after which time the position should be reviewed.," [28]he declared. On April 24 1956, the governor made a statement regarding elections. He said, "There will, I believe, be the general agreement in the House that the objective of our policy must be to introduce direct elections on a common roll for all representative members of LEGCO from all parts of the protectorate..." None of these objectives was achieved. It became apparent that the 1955 agreement had not solved the problem of Buganda as far as her inclination towards separatism was concerned. The Buganda Lukiko called on the Baganda members to resign from the Legislative Council. When two members of the United Congress Party resigned over the question of a common roll for future elections, they were not replaced. Differences of opinion between Buganda and the Colonial administration developed concerning Buganda's participation in the Legislative Council. The projected direct elections of Buganda Representatives to the Legislative Council were cancelled. The Mengo establishment reverted to the earlier demands that Buganda should be allowed to go its own way and demanded independence. When in 1957 the colonial office relented and agreed to hold direct elections to the Legislative Council throughout the country, Buganda declined to participate in the elections. True to British doctrine of divide and rule, the direct elections thus introduced were not compulsory. Each administrative unit was free to decide whether or not to opt for

Press 1961) p409.

28   *Despatch of Colonial Secretary No 692 of July 20, 1955.*

direct elections. In the event, only nine districts opted for direct elections, namely: Acholi, Bukedi, Bunyoro, Busoga, Kigezi, Lango, Teso, Toro, West Nile and Madi. Elections took place in October 1958. Ten directly elected members[29] were returned. The Uganda National Congress won four seats, the DP one seat and the independents claimed the rest. The number of independents were reinforced by two members indirectly elected by the Ishengyero (Ankole Kingdom Council). Many other districts decided to have indirect elections. Buganda, worried about her special status and the position of the Kabaka, declined to participate in the elections. The UNC group of four was headed by an upcoming politician, Apollo Milton Obote.

29   Directly elected Members were:
J. K. Babiiha, G. B. K. Magezi, C. J. Obwangor, A. M. Obote, B. K. Kirya, W. W. K. Nadiope, M. M. Ngobi, P. L. Oola, A. G. Bazanyamaso and Gaspare Oda

Chapter Nine

The Legislature At Work

It is appropriate at this juncture to examine the constitutional organs that were established to facilitate proper governance of the country. A study of political thought reveals that man has since the days of Aristotle sought to devise a foolproof political system that would guard against tyranny. The authors of the 1962 Constitution of Uganda made yet another attempt to achieve that end. The ultimate objective of the constitution was to ensure political stability, establishment of a free and open society with equal opportunities for all. The best way to achieve this objective, so they argued, was to define the functions of each branch of government, namely, the Legislature, the Executive and the Judiciary. However, the arrangement fell short of the United States model of separation of powers. The architects of the constitution kept in mind Madison's remarks: "The accumulation of powers in the same hands may justly be pronounced the very definition of tyranny".[30] "Power that is not in some fashion divided is bound to be absolute and power being, by its very nature, dangerous to those who exercise it, needs to be limited before it can be exercised with safety", adds Harold Laski in *Grammar of Politics*, . This analysis agrees with Montesquieu's famous statement: "When the Legislature and the Executive are united in the same person or body, there can be no liberty because apprehension may arise lest the same monarch or senate should enact tyrannical laws, to enforce them in a tyrannical manner. Were the powers of judging joined with the Legislature, the life and liberty of the

30   *Madison James: Federalist, No 46 (ed. Ford)* PP 319.

subject would be exposed to arbitrary control for the judge would then be the legislator. Were it joined to the Executive power, the judge might behave with all the violence of an oppressor"[31] As expected, of the three branches of government the Legislature proved to be the most popular with the population. It was one visible sign of democracy.

It is, therefore, necessary to devote a few lines on the functions of the National Assembly during the first three years of its existence. Article 74 of the 1962 Constitution stipulated that "Parliament shall have sole power to make laws for the peace, order and good government of Uganda with respect to any matter". At the same time the Legislatures of the kingdoms of Ankole, Buganda, Bunyoro, Toro, and of the Territory of Busoga were empowered to make laws in respect of certain specified matters provided such laws were not inconsistent with the enactment of Parliament.

In order to facilitate effective legislation, elaborate machinery was enshrined in the Constitution. The machinery or organs consisted of the National Assembly and the Office of the Head of State. The National Assembly was composed of eighty-two elected members and nine specially elected members bringing the total number to ninety one. In addition, if a person who was not a member of National Assembly was appointed to the office of the Attorney General of Uganda or elected to the office of the Speaker of the National Assembly, that person was deemed to be a member of the National Assembly by virtue of his office.

The Constitution provided for the National Assembly to regulate its own procedure. The Standing Orders dealt with such diverse subjects as the administration of the oath of allegiance to Members, the powers of the Speaker, a Code of Conduct to be observed within the Assembly chamber, procedures regarding parliamentary business such as questions, motions and bills. The Standing Orders also dealt with the appointment of sessional and select committees and such incidental matters that were necessary for the effective exercise of legislative powers. The Standing Orders of the National Assembly encouraged precision; and precision has the world over been the hallmark of the rules of debate. The effect of the Standing Orders was that all discussion and all debate should be relevant to a motion of which notice was almost invariably required to be given. So, all motions had to be cast in a form that expressed the opinion or the will of the National Assembly. The Motion had to be capable of being amended, capable of being voted upon so that at the end of the debate everyone knew exactly what was decided by the Assembly.

31   *Esprit des lais* Bk X1 chapter V1.

The rules of debate and etiquette protected a member from unnecessary interruptions and made business of the National Assembly to proceed with decorum and dignity. There were three main functions of Parliament, namely, Legislation, Control of Public Funds, and the Ventilation of Grievances. A brief description of each of these functions will suffice.

Articles 63 and 58 of the 1962 Constitution read as follows: "Subject to the provisions of this Constitution, Parliament shall have sole power to make laws for the peace, order and good government of Uganda with respect to any matter. The power of Parliament to make laws shall be exercised by bills passed by the national Assembly and assented to by the President."

In the discharge of Parliament's first function, it was the government, which played the leading role by taking the initiative. By government here is meant Cabinet. Most of the legislation took the form of bills embodying the principles of the successful political party and the promises made in its manifesto. In the first instance, every bill brought to the National Assembly had to be published in the Uganda Gazette. It bore an explanatory memorandum, couched in a layman's language, of the aims, objectives and the effect of the bill. The memorandum did not form part of the law when the bill was ultimately passed by Parliament. Every bill consisted of a long title, which was actually the name of the bill or reference. There was also an enacting formula, which read: "<u>Be it enacted by the President and the National Assembly assembled as</u> <u>follows</u>". Then there was the main body which bore a head note or a side note. In some bills there were schedules which gave greater details in respect of a given clause. All bills were introduced into the House by government. However, there was nothing to prevent a private member introducing a bill if he had the time and resources to do so. Every bill went through certain stages before it became law. According to Standing Orders, the bill went through four stages: First Reading, Second Reading, Committee Stage and the Third Reading. The progress of bills was spelt out under Standing Orders 59 – 74 of the National Assembly. The main debate took place during the second reading. This was the stage when the principles of the bill were discussed while the committee stage was meant for details. After the second reading, the bill went to the Committee of the whole House where it was considered clause by clause in a more relaxed atmosphere. Members could speak more than once to any motion. The Clerk read out the clauses one by one. It was usually at that stage that amendments were moved. In certain cases when a bill proved to be controversial, it could be referred to a

Select Committee. The Select Committee then considered the bill in great detail. The Select Committee could, if it deemed it necessary, interview members of the public or various interest groups to ascertain their views. The strength of the House was always reflected in the membership of the Select Committees[32] so that the government maintained a majority. After a series of meetings, the Committee made a report which was submitted to the whole House upon a motion: "That the report of the Select Committee be approved". After the bill was passed by the House, the Clerk of the National Assembly sent a copy with or without amendment as the case might be to the Parliamentary Counsel in the Attorney General's Chambers, who in turn prepared four assent copies for the signature of the President. The officer in charge of this schedule of duty was designated Parliamentary Counsel. He kept in constant touch with the Clerk to the national assembly on all legislative matters. The bill then became an Act of Parliament and was published as such in the Uganda Gazette. It is important to note at this juncture that one of the main aspects of parliamentary democracy – the element of the rule of law, is that, only Parliament could make laws or dispense with laws. It is also interesting to note that while the Opposition could vote against a bill, once that bill became law, it was binding on everybody. Hence the saying, "The minority must have its say, but the majority must have its way". Every government has to raise and spend money. Government may have excellent plans but plans cannot be implemented without financial backing. Even if money is available, it is vital to have reasonable control of the finances at all levels because few things undermine the people's faith in an administration's ability and efficiency more than the knowledge that the system employed lends itself to needless waste or opens the door to corruption. It is, therefore, imperative that government should adopt methods that will contain safeguards against evils of corruption. But safeguards alone are not enough and in the interests of the country, something more is necessary. It is not enough for government to know an estimated expenditure on a given project because it may be persuaded to spend more than say the country can afford. Further safeguards are therefore desirable to prevent government from over-straining the economy, discouraging the expansion of the industry and commerce and at times discouraging incentive by over-

32   Select Committee:
A select committee may be appointed at any time by the House for a great variety of purposes, the usual purpose is that of considering or enquiring into a certain given matter and reporting back their opinion or findings on the matter to enable the House take appropriate action.

taxation. Real power rests with those who control taxation. It was for that reason that there was a special provision in the Constitution to the effect that the government should initiate all financial measures.

A word about the Draft Annual estimates and Expenditure: in December or thereabouts of every year, the Ministry of Finance would send a circular to all government ministries and departments. The circular sought submission of estimates of each Department for the next financial year. The financial year ran from July 1st to 30th June. One by one, ministries submitted their estimates for both Recurrent and Development Expenditure. A great deal of consultation went on within the ministry among the departments and sections. Then officials of every ministry met with officials of the Ministry of Finance to iron out differences and defend submissions made by their respective ministries. In cases where officials of a given ministry did not reach an accord with the officials of the Ministry of Finance, the differences were referred to the Ministers concerned to settle. Consultations continued until say April, when the Ministry of Finance started compiling the estimates under their appropriate headings. By that time, the Treasury would have three sets of figures: the total expenditure of the current financial year, the total amount of revenue it expected to raise for the following financial year and the total estimated expenditure of the new financial year. The ministry was then in a position to know whether to expect a surplus or a deficit. Armed with that information, the Minister of Finance then moved swiftly and started working on the budget proposals. In doing so he usually looked at the general state of the national economy. The previous year may have been a stagnant one for say industry or the country may have experienced adverse balance of payments. On the other hand, the previous year may have experienced an economic boom with an unexpected rise in revenue from unexpected areas of the economy. Those were matters that the minister had to take into account when he considered budget proposals for the following year.

After putting the final touches in the morning of the budget day, the minister gave a comprehensive brief to the cabinet. By convention members of cabinet proceeded to the National Assembly immediately after the brief to hear the budget speech. In his speech, the Minister of Finance usually reviewed the public finances and economic position of the country. He did that for the benefit of Members of Parliament so that they would be aware of the difficulties that might have arisen during the past year over say exports and balance of payments and how industry and commerce were progressing generally. He could choose to say something about existing taxes and their yields.

In the course of his speech the minister indicated how much of the proposed revenue for the coming year he proposed to raise by taxation and how much by loan. Finally, came the climax, the actual taxation proposals-Standing order 75 dealt with the procedure in respect of Annual Estimates, supplementary estimates and the Vote on Account. Debate on the budget speech was adjourned for a number of days as decided by the Standing Committee on Rules and Orders to allow members to study and digest the speech. When the debate resumed it was limited to a specified number of days. That formed a general debate on the general state of the economy. Then the House proceeded to debate individual votes whereby every minister responsible for the selected votes was called upon to initiate a debate under his vote by making a policy statement. Each vote so selected was allotted a number of days in such a way that the total of days taken to consider the annual estimates did not exceed the approved days set aside for the purpose. After every mini debate under a given vote, the House resolved itself into a committee of supply and proceeded to consider the particular vote in detail by examining the vote item by item. The process continued until all the votes so selected were dealt with. But if by the last allotted day the House had not completed discussion of all the votes, the speaker applied a guillotine to ensure that the annual estimates were approved before the expiration of the specified period.

In the committee of the whole house members were allowed to speak more than once and could move amendments to reduce the vote. Moving an amendment was a technical way through which a member could show his displeasure or dissatisfaction with a given line ministry performance. In that way Parliament was able to scrutinise the annual estimates and later to satisfy itself whether or not the funds voted by the House were spent on the purposes for which the money was voted. That was done through one of parliament's most powerful committees-the Public Accounts Committee which had the right to study, to discuss and to probe the Report of the Auditor General. In those days the Auditor general was regarded as an official of Parliament and was quite independent of the executive arm of government.

The Committee had powers to summon any person it deemed necessary to interrogate. It was usually the Permanent Secretaries in their capacity as Accounting Officers who were called upon to give evidence to the Committee. By tradition, the Chairman of the Committee was drawn from the Opposition. The 1995 Constitution empowers Parliament to take an active part in the budgeting process through one of its Standing Committees rather than simply carrying out a fiscal post-mortem.

One other function of the House was ventilation of grievances. A member could ventilate his grievances or that of the people he represented in a number of ways. The most popular one was by parliamentary questions. Another method was by a motion for adjournment of the House, which in most cases arose out of an unsatisfactory reply to a question by a member. The extreme case was a motion of no confidence in the government. None was ever moved.

Chapter Ten

Political Stability And Development

"We are servants of the law in order that we may be free"
(Cicero).

We have seen the developments and progress of the political party system. By the end of 1959 the prospects for establishing a two party system were bright. A.M. Obote had emerged as an undisputed leader of the newly formed party, the Uganda Peoples Congress. His emergence as a new leader aroused mixed feelings from certain quarters, but for once Ugandan politicians agreed to bury the hatchet. Political and personal ambitions were suppressed, if not submerged. All this was done in order to achieve independence for Uganda. Independence had really never been in doubt. What was at issue was the timing. Buganda and the Agreement kingdoms could have caused a problem by putting off the date for independence. The adoption of the Munster Report on the future relationships between the central government, the kingdoms and the districts paved the way for independence. That was a great compromise.

From October 1962 Uganda entered what I may call its only golden era so far. An elected government was in place. There was a parliament whose majority was directly elected. There was a recognised parliamentary opposition with Basil Bataringaya as its leader. Government backbench members formed themselves into a strong parliamentary lobby that no cabinet minister could ignore. The principles of collective responsibility and ministerial accountability to parliament were recognised. The population as a whole was kept well-informed about government policies and actions through parliament. Buganda, which for a long time was reluctant to play a meaningful role in the national affairs of the country, became a junior partner in the government of the day. As a matter of fact, Kabaka Yekka ministers held key positions in the cabinet and wielded great influence. Amos Sempa, J.T Simpson, Joshua Zake, Kalule Settala and Dr. Emmanuel Lumu held the portfolios of Finance, Economic Development, Education, Works and Health, respectively. All major nationalities were adequately represented in the cabinet. The three major branches of government, the Executive, the Legislature and the Judiciary were discharging their responsibilities in strict adherence to the constitution in which their powers were well-defined. There was respect for the rule of law. The country's political leadership appeared to agree with Cicero when he says, *"We are servants of the law in order that we may be free"*. The country was moving towards constitutionalism and democratic governance in pursuit of progress, stability and individual freedom. The objective was for all Ugandans to pull together and build a community spirit more than individualism and hope more than negation. The trend was to choose equality of opportunities and avoid greed. To that end a call went out to every Ugandan to join the battle for a better future for all, which alone justified the efforts and change of heart. In the interest of political stability peace and national unity the Kabaka of Buganda, Sir Edward Mutesa II, was appointed by Parliament at the instigation of the Prime Minister to the high office of the President of Uganda. He replaced the British Governor-General. Sir William Wilberforce Kajumbula Nadiope, Busoga's traditional Ruler, became Vice President. Unfortunately, the new set up did not eliminate completely the dangers of factionalism that everybody had worked so hard to eradicate. Nevertheless, until things fell apart there was a marked sense of national consciousness. There was also a spirit of fraternity, never experienced before, throughout the country.

The Economy

> *"We have to pursue the science of managing our own house, the earth, we do not own the world's wealth; we hold it on loan from our ancestors and in trust for our children." (United Nations General Secretary, Boutros Butros-Ghali, 1992 Rio Conference on Environment and Development)*

In the field of commerce and industry the government made concerted efforts in the 1960s to correct the legacy of British paternalism in commerce by increasing the African share of the wholesale and retail trade. Government established the African Business Promotion Unit in 1963 followed by the National Trading Corporation(NTC) in 1966. Due to a number of reasons like ineptitude, nepotism and outright corruption, the NTC failed. In 1969 Parliament passed the Trade Licensing Act, which empowered the government to reserve certain business centres for the exclusive use by citizens thus placing restrictions on the commercial activities of non-citizens, especially those engaged in retail trade. To complete the process, necessary measures were put in place. The 1969 Bank Act required all existing commercial banks to be incorporated locally and maintain a cash capital of a certain amount.

The government adopted certain economic measures that aimed at achieving an average growth rate of 3.5% and possibly accelerate to 5% by the end of the five-year period. The First Five-Year plan laid the foundation for a more rapid growth in the future. The effort of government was to completely transform the economic and social structure of Uganda in the shortest possible time. It was to double the monetary income per capita from roughly $25 to $50 by the year 1981. Because of the anticipated population increase over that period and in order to maintain constant economic growth rate, it was imperative to aim at trebling the total output within a period of 15 years. I must hasten to add that the economic programme was not solely concerned with merely increasing national income. Far from it, there was great concern for the need to strike out an equitable distribution of that national income (the national cake) and make adequate provision for social services, namely, health and education. The government saw or regarded itself as trustees of the people of Uganda irrespective of "nationality", creed or colour. Strategies to achieve these objectives were embodied in the Second Five-Year Plan (1966-71). The main target areas were agriculture, industry and education. Uganda with her political upheavals notwithstanding had one of the best resource endowed economies south of the Sahara particularly in the agricultural sector. During the 1960s Uganda made a concerted effort to exploit to the full these potentials. As a result, the country was self-sufficient in food and exported large quantities of coffee, cotton, tea, sugar and tobacco. Since 90% of the population were engaged in farming, agricultural development was designed to encompass the mass of the population so that they could effectively contribute to the economy and thereby participate in the benefits of development. The plan also envisaged that with the rise of income accruing from economic development, the demand for goods that make life worthwhile, most of which were imported, would expand very fast. Something had to be done to meet the anticipated increased demand and move away or at least reduce the degree of dependence on foreign sources of supply. It was necessary to step up the tempo of industrialisation. The two strategies required trained and skilled manpower. Hence, there was a need to develop and expand educational facilities. The government set out to achieve these targets by embarking on the expansion of industrial production through the aegis of the Uganda Development Corporation that was floated with a capital of 5million pounds drawn entirely from local funds and established in 1952 for purposes of stimulating industrialisation. By 1968, the UDC had 39 subsidiary and associated companies each with its own specialised management. Some of the subsidiaries were Nyanza Textile Industries, Uganda Cement Industry, Tororo Industrial and Chemical Fertilisers, Kilembe Mines, Agricultural Enterprises, Lango Spinning Mill, Uganda Hotels Ltd, East African Distilleries, Uganda Metal Products and Enamel Company. Most of these enterprises have since been sold off to foreigners. We shall deal with that later.

The government also took appropriate measures to encourage both foreign and local participation in the industrialisation process. To that effect, the Foreign Investment Act was passed by Parliament in 1964. There were other laws that gave incentives to foreign investors. At the same time, government took steps to encourage greater participation by indigenous Africans in industry. The Management Training and Advisory Centre was established in 1966 with the assistance of two agencies of the United Nations (ILO and UNDP). The role of the Centre was to train small industrial entrepreneurs in new techniques and in business management and to help them set up and operate small industrial establishments.

An area in which the government made the greatest impact was Animal Industry. By 1968 there were 3.9 million head of cattle and 3.5 million goats and sheep in the country, *1967 Livestock Census*. Under the guidance and able leadership of the Minister of Animal Game and Fisheries, John K. Babiha, there was a dramatic increase of milk production. A Diary Industry Corporation was set up to process milk supplied by farmers from all over the country. By the end of the 1960s Uganda, which had for a long time depended on Kenya for the supply of fresh milk, had attained self-sufficiency. Following an extensive eradication of tsetse flies, several ranches were established under government extension schemes. In this respect, even Peter M. Gukiina, who describes Amin as a national symbol of unity, peace and social justice, acknowledges thus: "It was remarkable that through modern ranching schemes and government milk cooling processing, programmes in cattle grazing areas had almost tripled milk production in the country in eight years". He goes on to say, "The government efforts in this area are highly commendable when one realises that successful import substitution of milk, meat, cream, butter, ghee and cheese alone meant total savings of $8,500,000 in foreign exchange": *Uganda, a case study in African political development* (P154-155).

Whatever the detractors may say or write, it is a fact that by the time of the military take over in 1971 Uganda boasted of a small dynamic industrial base with a well-developed communications infrastructure. The country had a well-diversified economy with subsistence production accounting for no more than 30% of the total output. Poultry industry began to take root and high quality eggs came on the market while the production of hides and skins was stepped up. These industries continued to be the source of income until the harsh economic conditions experienced during the Amin period of the economic war and the SAP regime imposed by the World Bank economic strategies in the late 1980s.

Ugandans were able to make savings, which averaged 15%. "It was then possible to finance internal investment so that the economy was not seriously constrained by the balance of payments and inflation. Export earnings covered import requirements adequately and the country enjoyed a current account- surplus in most years. By 1970, Uganda had net reserves equivalent to four months of imports."[33] However, the state of the economy drastically changed after 1971 due to domestic and external shocks. Internally, the country lost skilled manpower and competent managers were subjected to an exploitative administrative system. The global increase of petroleum prices and later the collapse of the East African Community drove in the last nail in Uganda's economy. It ground to a halt.

In the field of Education and Health, Uganda had built an impressive network of social services. There were hospitals both in urban and rural areas. By 1970 all the new twenty-one hospitals had been completed and fully equipped. There were dispensaries, health centres, schools and technical colleges. Mulago Hospital the largest hospital was Uganda's showpiece and its standard rivalled those of any hospital in Africa. What is important to remember is that all the hospitals including dispensaries and aid posts were functional. Doctors, nurses and auxiliary staff enjoyed a living wage. Service to the population was guaranteed.

---

33   Government of Uganda.*Investment Programme 1982-84.*

The UPC leadership believed and continues to believe more than ever before in Plato's dictum that man is the measure of all things. Accordingly, the UPC government invested heavily in education at all levels including adult education. To be able to achieve industrialisation and modernising the economy, it was incumbent upon the government of the day to seriously address the question of education. Primary school enrolment went up from 434,995 pupils in 1962 to 641,639 in 1967. For secondary schools, the intake rose from 9.400 to 27,025 in 1967. (*Facts about Uganda 1968, Ministry of Information):* Technical schools were expanded to cater for the training technicians in building, carpentry, electrical installation, plumbing and other skills. Teacher training colleges were expanded to allow greater intake to be able to cope with increased demand for trained teachers. In addition, there were two other colleges of further education, the Uganda Technical College and the Uganda College of Commerce. These two institutions were very crucial at the time. The former was meant to produce technicians who in any developing country are destined to play a vital role in modernisation, while the college of commerce was called upon to turn out professionals in the field of accountancy to man government departments and assist the private sector. It will be recalled that at that time the profession was dominated by non- Ugandans. So, it was important to take the lead in training local people in that discipline.

One of the main factors that contributed to political stability during the three year golden period under review i.e. 1962-65, was the willingness of the majority political party in Parliament to accept and tolerate views held or expressed by the minority party. In other words, the system permitted political parties and other interest groups to freely exist as separate entities and to carry out political activities in pursuit of achieving the aims and objectives for which their organisations stood. In the Legislature the Opposition Party was officially recognised and had the right not only to oppose and to criticise government policies when the occasion arose but was in fact encouraged to do so.

There was a Leader of the Opposition who enjoyed the benefits pertaining to that office. Members of the Opposition were involved in the transaction of all National Assembly business. The opposition was represented on all sessional and select committees of the House. The membership of these committees reflected the percentage of the respective numerical strength of the parties in the House. In the case of the Public Accounts Committee, the convention of the British House Of Commons was followed whereby the chairman was invariably nominated from the

Opposition. The late Hon. A.A Latim was the chairman. That arrangement provided greater opportunity for the opposition to carry out a meaningful inquisition into the expenditure of public funds by the government. The system was meant to ensure government financial accountability to the legislature. The practice was that the committee would take evidence under the cover of confidentiality and submit a report to Parliament with appropriate recommendations where irregularities were uncovered.

The Executive through the Treasury would take necessary action by causing police investigation or taking administrative action. Cases of fraud, embezzlement or outright theft would be referred to the police to initiate prosecution. Unlike the National Resistance Council or the Parliament under the 1995 Constitution, it was not for the legislature to pass judgement or impose punishment. Laid down procedures were followed. The system worked well mainly because there was respect for the rule of law all round. The elected political government (for the period 62-65) shunned public scandals. Public officers were well motivated and accounting officers (permanent secretaries) enjoyed public esteem. They saw no reason why they should not enforce financial restrictions and instructions to the letter. Most of them could not be easily intimidated by politicians because there was security of tenure of office. Dismissal of established government officials through the media and outside laid down procedures was not part of the civil service culture. That type of practice emerged with the advent of military dictatorship. Prior to this the Public Service Commission was safely insulated from the pressures and control of the Executive.

However, the degree of the independence of the commission rested on the personality of the Chairman of the Commission. That of course is no longer the case today. In short, corruption had not yet permeated the body politic of Ugandan society. Throughout the first three years of independence good relations and co-operation flourished between the government and the opposition. Much of the credit of that cordial relationship goes to two persons, namely, the late Basil Bataringaya and Cuthbert Obwangor who did their utmost to ensure a smooth running of the business of the House. The former was the leader of the opposition and the latter was the leader of government business.

A great deal has been written and said about the late Basil Bataringaya. A few more words of tribute would not be out of place. Basil Bataringaya became leader of the Opposition in the House following the defeat of the Democratic Party in the April 1962 elections. Benedicto Kiwanuka,

President General of the party, had no means of finding his way to parliament. The Buganda kingdom preferred to have the twenty-one parliamentary seats filled by indirect election through the Lukiko serving as an electoral college. Buganda's "wish" was endorsed by the majority of the delegates at the September 1961 London conference. That endorsement which was later embodied in the 1962 Uganda constitution sealed Benedicto Kiwanuka's political fate. He found himself together with his top officials from Buganda in the political wilderness. Because the political party system was not deeply rooted and well-established it was not possible for the DP President General to stand for election outside Buganda.

Ideally, a DP Member of parliament from outside Buganda could have resigned his seat and offered it to his boss in a by election. The Indian National Congress applied that device to get Mrs Indira Gandhi to Parliament after her defeat in the general election in her local constituency. In Uganda, nationality or ethnic cleavages were still too strong to permit such an arrangement. There is, however, no evidence that after forty years of independence the situation has changed!

Nevertheless, such were the circumstances under which the late Basil Bataringaya assumed the role of the leader of the Opposition in Uganda's parliament. What type of man was he? He was intelligent, articulate, supple, conciliating and infinitely persuasive. His gift for political manoeuvre secured his passage to government benches without rancour. In this respect he was a towering figure within the DP rank and file. He was genial in his relations with his fellow members of parliament and courteous in his general conduct of behaviour. He was quick witted and an excellent debater in the House. There was something special about him. He had vision- a vivid perspective for Uganda. In other words, for him Uganda transcended other organisations. He was a nationalist. His performance in the House was undoubtedly above average. The Democratic Party supporters expected him to take over leadership of the party as a whole, but his political boss was not prepared to step down. A rift between the DP parliamentary group and the DP executive developed. When the Kabaka Yekka/ Uganda Peoples Congress alliance collapsed, Bataringaya and his group saw avenues of serving the country from government benches. They joined the governing party. I am not convinced, as alleged from some quarters, that they were lured to the government benches by the rewards of office. What I know is that Bataringaya's move enabled the experiment in parliamentary democracy to continue for a while in spite of the determined effort of the reactionary forces to dispense with the democratisation process.

Chapter Eleven

Power Struggle And The Political Storm

"I have thought it proper to represent things as they are in real truth, rather than they are imagined" (Niccolo Machiavelli).

The accession to power by the Uganda Peoples Congress created new problems for the Party. The party began experiencing internal friction.

Struggle for power raised its ugly head. First of all, there was controversy over ideology which split the ruling party, leading to a direct conflict between the Party's General Secretary and a factional group. The alliance between Uganda People's Congress and the Kabaka Yekka helped strengthen the factional group. John Kakonge was the first victim of the re-alignment of forces within the alliance. He was excluded from the National Assembly after the 1962 elections. John Kakonge did not stand for elections on the understanding that he would get one of the nine specially elected seats. That avenue was denied to him mainly through intrigues and trappings of a prominent member of the ruling party. The failure to enter parliament was one of the outstanding blows John Kakonge suffered in the whole of his political career. He was so distressed and disgusted that he fled to Tanzania to seek consolation and refuge from Mwalimu Nyerere. Nine years later, the president of the Uganda Peoples Congress went through a similar experience following the military coup in 1971. Several years earlier, Kabaka Mwanga had also taken refuge in Tanganyika. The nefarious strategy of permanently excluding Kakonge from parliament by his political opponents was followed by a new scheme which entailed ousting him from his position as Secretary-General of the party. The year was 1964. The venue was Pece Sports stadium, now renamed Kaunda stadium, Gulu. The occasion was the annual delegates' conference. I hate going through the narrative of the crude and ruthless method employed for Kakonge's ouster. It was ugly. There was bribery, intimidation and all sorts of irregularities. The upshot was that Grace Ibingira became Secretary-General of the party.

The delegates invited to the annual conference consisted of representatives from the then existing districts of Uganda. There were sixteen districts, namely, Acholi, Ankole, Bugisu, Bukedi, Bunyoro, Busoga, East Mengo, Karamoja, Kigezi, Lango, Masaka, Mubende, Teso, Toro, West Mengo, and West Nile. The numerical strength of each district delegation depended on the population of the district. That is why Buganda, which consisted of East Mengo, Masaka, Mubende and West Mengo had the biggest delegation. Buganda was followed by Busoga and Bukedi, in that order. According to the provisions of the party constitution, the total number of delegates could not have legally exceeded one thousand. When the accredited delegates arrived in Gulu, the general feeling was that the majority of delegates were firmly behind John Kakonge. They were gearing to re-elect him to the post of Secretary-General. The president of the party who was the country's Prime Minister favoured Grace Ibingira who had the support of most of the cabinet ministers. The ministers who went out of their way to block the re-election of John Kakonge included Balaki K. Kirya, Felix Onama, Adoko Nekyon, Vice President Wilberforce Nadiope and Dr. Emmanuel Lumu. A victory for Kakonge would have been a great embarrassment and humiliation to the Prime Minister and his Cabinet. It was therefore decided to postpone the inauguration of the conference for a day. Balaki Kirya was dispatched to the government printer in Entebbe by helicopter. His mission was simple; to get extra accreditation cards printed to cater for the "unofficial delegates" as a counter balance against Kakonge's overwhelming support. Earlier on an unsuccessful attempt was made to disqualify some delegates from Buganda as they were supposed to be Kakonge's supporters. Binaisa's group was for Kakonge while Lumu's faction was in the opposite camp. In the end it was 'Vice President Nadiope's delegates from Busoga who tipped the balance against the incumbent Secretary-General. Sir Wilberforce Nadiope had to travel back to Kampala to organise the recruitment of an extra three hundred delegates.

Finally, the conference began at about three O'clock in the afternoon and continued until three O'clock in the morning. The significance of the meeting was the way it was conducted. The agenda was unceremoniously changed. The original agenda was to feature a speech by the Secretary-General who in the course of his speech was to invite the president of the party to address the delegates. That was to be followed by the presentation of accounts and related financial matters by the treasurer. All that was altered for the convenience of the aspirant candidate for the post of Secretary-General. In fact, only two items were dealt with at the conference- the speech by the President of the party and elections which started past midnight. The outcome of the elections was as predicted; Grace Ibingira, Minister of Justice became the new Secretary-General. It was quite remarkable that despite the rigging and other mal-practices, Ibingira won the election by a slim margin. John Kakonge's supporters demanded a recount of the votes or better still a re-run of the elections. However, all that fell on deaf ears. Adoko Nekyon and Felix Onama who were the returning officers could not hear of it. Tension was extremely high among the delegates. The following day youth leaders convened a meeting at which John Kakonge was urged to break away from the parent party and form a new one. In his own characteristic way Kakonge addressed the youth leaders and persuaded them to call off the move to split the "Congress of the People". Therein, lay Kakonge's greatest gift – self-sacrifice for the good of the nation and the Party.

The Gulu events had serious repercussions for the future politics of Uganda. Among the first actions taken by the new Secretary-General was to purge the staff at the Party's Headquarters. Since that time the secretariat has never been effective in terms of generating ideas, resourcefulness and organisational capacity.

Kakonge's ouster signalled the start of a struggle for state power. The newly elected Secretary-General aligned himself with powerful men in government positions. The powerful men included the President and Vice President of Uganda. He also enjoyed appreciable support in cabinet thus making it difficult for the Prime Minister and the government as a whole to function in harmony and effectively. Hard-pressed, A.M Obote retracted his steps. He rehabilitated the former General-Secretary. By some discreet arrangement, Paulo Muwanga, a specially elected member resigned his seat and was appointed Uganda's ambassador to the United Arab Republic (Egypt). Muwanga's exit made room for John Kakonge to get into parliament. He was duly sworn in on May 31, 1965. In August of that year KY/UPC alliance collapsed.

John Kakonge devoted the greater and best part of his life to the service of Uganda. He played a key role during the formative days of the Uganda People's Congress. He had just returned in the late 1950s from overseas studies with a Master's degree in Economics. Unlike the British trained youths of his days whether educated locally at Makerere University or in Great Britain (many regarded Britain as their home) he plunged himself into active politics straight away. He thus brought a new dimension into the politics of Uganda. Hitherto, young graduates shunned active politics. He was soon joined by a smaller group of other graduates. They were all Indian-trained.

When India attained Independence, Prime Minister Jawaharlal Nehru, opened the doors of his country's universities under a special scheme to Third World students, especially those from Africa. John Kakonge was awarded one of those scholarships. He obtained his first degree at Jaipur University and then took up Economics at the Delhi School of Economics. Delhi School of Economics is a college of the University of Delhi, one of the finest universities in the Commonwealth of Nations. It is still India's showpiece.

His tireless and selfless devotion to the Uganda People's Congress soon won him admiration not only from congressmen but also from his political opponents. In 1961 he became Secretary-General of the party in recognition of his ability and hard work. He won a seat to the legislative council in the 1961 elections. He was thus firmly established in the leadership of the Uganda People's Congress. While in India he was closely associated with the All India National Congress, the African Students Association and the Uganda Students Association in India. All those associations aimed at establishing social justice and the elimination of colonialism. He therefore easily understood power politics, international relations and, above all, the evils of colonialism and imperialism. To him religion was as it should be, a personal matter, while tribalism was a thing of the past. Nationalism transcended everything else. All his energy, intellect and time were devoted to the creation of a strong independent Uganda based on freedom, enlightened leadership, equality of opportunity and the projection of the image of the African and human dignity. He knew what constituted a national political party. What is more, he knew how to go about setting up the necessary machinery for its organisation.

Human nature being what it is, some of his colleagues began to be jealous of him. They grew restless as the time of independence drew near. He was branded a communist. Socialism and communism preoccupied his rivals. Worse still, the fact that John Kakonge was young, dynamic and educated, did not please them.

In his book, *Uganda the Crisis of Confidence*, Kirunda Kivejinja, one of Kakonge's recruits wants people to believe that John Kakonge was naïve when he says , 'Kakonge's naiveté were such that clues the size of a mountain would be required to make him suspect the slightest figment of a trick'. That obviously is an uneducated description of Kakonge. John was full of confidence with a great deal of a fighting spirit and believed that time was on his side. He was also a protagonist of dialogue as an instrument of conflict resolution. He detested confrontation and violence. Above all, it was natural for him to assume a stature of dignity and due composure whenever he felt he was being undermined. Opportunism rarely found room in his vocabulary.

John's perception of political developments can be illustrated by the way he reacted to Daudi Ochieng's motion of February 4, 1966. He read correctly the strategy of Ochieng's cohort and challenged them to move a motion of no confidence in the government. He actually told the House that the motion was a mere ploy to get rid of Amin who was the only obstacle standing in their way to State House. This was not a manifestation of naivety.

The honeymoon following the alliance between the Uganda People's Congress and Kabaka Yekka was short-lived. By the year 1964, great strains between the two partners had developed. It is difficult to put the sequence of events in its proper perspective. The driving force and the political motives behind the alliance have been dealt with in the preceding pages. Suffice to give a background of the break up of the alliance. It will be recalled that one of the most controversial issues that were latent and likely to wreck the pre-independence London conference was the dispute over the "lost counties". However, an agreement was reached which stipulated that a referendum would be held in two of the six counties. The referendum was to take place not less than two years after independence. That such an arrangement was agreed upon by all parties concerned was a great achievement for Uganda. It was also proof of the spirit of give and take which characterised the talks at the conference. The participants were determined that nothing should delay independence. By the same token the UPC had earlier on gone an extra mile to accommodate Mengo after the latter's unilateral declaration of independence on December 31, 1960.

What was the political implication of the decision to hold a referendum in Buyaga and Bugangaizi? To those who were politically conscious, the decision was a great victory for democracy. It was a manifestation that Uganda had embarked on a long but arduous road to democratisation. The conference recognised that the dispute was basically not between the Omukama of Bunyoro and the Kabaka of Buganda, but a claim based on the inhabitants' aspirations. The device of a referendum was to provide an opportunity to the people concerned to express their political will. At bottom, it was an acknowledgement of the principle of self-determination.

What effect did such a fundamental matter of principle have on the newly formed alliance between the Uganda Peoples Congress and Kabaka Yekka? The idea of a referendum cut across the very principles upon which the Kabaka Yekka political organisation was established. The organisation was established to protect and defend the Kabakaship and the kingdom. It may be recalled that Kabakaship as an institution was hereditary. The organisation had nothing to do with democracy. The KY was opposed to direct elections of Buganda's representatives to the National Assembly. Members of parliament from Buganda had one and only one constituency, the Lukiko that served as an electoral college. The Mengo establishment saw no merit in a multi-party political system. All national political parties, including the Uganda Peoples Congress, were not allowed to operate freely in Buganda.

It was no wonder then that the holding of a referendum in the two counties of Buyaga and Bugangaizi played a big part in the collapse of the alliance. It was also one of the reasons that drew the Mengo clique and its supporters closer to the group within the UPC that was scheming against the Prime Minister's leadership. When the Prime Minister finally made up his mind that the provisions of the 1962 constitution regarding the lost counties' settlement should be implemented, he was condemned as dishonest and treacherous. It was argued that if the political leadership in Mengo had any respect for the country's constitution and other public institutions like the High Court, the events of 1966 might not have taken place. For the rest of Uganda, the holding of the referendum was an occasion to test the degree of Mengo's commitment to the development of democratic processes in all aspects of political life. It was a test to prove that all Ugandans would let bygones be bygones: that kings, princes, workers and peasants alike could live together in amity. Everybody was expected to strive and create a new and prosperous Uganda. That was not the case. The reactionary elements were against change. They thought of the privileges they had enjoyed during the colonial era and were determined to halt the march of progress towards a genuine democratic system. The Buganda establishment did not stop at terrorising the long-suffering inhabitants of Buyaga and Bugangaizi but hatched plans to frustrate the process of the proposed referendum. The Ndaiga settlement scheme was established in 1963. Under the scheme over four thousand men were settled in the two counties. Most of the settlers were *kawonawo* (veterans of the two world wars). It must be emphasised that the scheme was very close to the heart of Sir Edward Mutesa, who at that material time was President of the whole country. As such, he was supposed to be a symbol of unity and a source of inspiration for the young nation. He spent a great deal of time at Ndaiga, despite his pressing presidential duties at State House. The Ndaiga scheme, which came to be known as an investment of no return, was a genesis of vote rigging in Uganda's body politic- not much of an inspiration from somebody holding the highest office in the land. A lot of public funds were spent on the scheme and accountability was hard to come by. Indeed, the central government accused the Buganda administration personnel of being involved in embezzlement of funds. All that took place before the scheduled referendum. Mengo's illegal activities and machinations did not deter the Central Government from discharging its obligation. Accordingly, on August 25, 1964, the Minister of Justice, C. J. Obwangor, moved a motion in the following terms: "Resolved that this House, in accordance with the provisions of paragraph (a) of sub section (1) of section 26 of the Uganda independence order in council 1962, do hereby appoint the day of 4th November 1964, as the date on which the referendum to ascertain the wishes of the inhabitants of the counties of Buyaga and Bugangaizi, as to the territory in Uganda in which each of the counties should be included, shall take place."

During the course of the debate members of Parliament belonging to the Kabaka Yekka walked out of the chamber in protest. Three days later, that is, on August 28, 1964, the Referundum (Buyaga and Bugangaizi) Bill 1964 was introduced in the House and passed. The Bill was supported by both sides of the House. The Leader of the Opposition stressed the need for strict observance of the Constitution "to which we are committed". Paulo Muwanga, who was a backbencher scoffed at the walking out of the Chamber by the Kabaka Yekka members. He pointed out that the remedy for any aggrieved party was to go to Court. C. J. Magara, Member of Parliament for Bunyoro South West echoed the views expressed by previous speakers. M.K. Kuhikya, member of Parliament for Bunyoro north-east called for stringent security measures to be put in place to ensure law and order on the referendum day.

There was one sticky issue; a bill passed by parliament does not automatically become law. The last stage in the process of legislation requires that the assent copy of the bill be signed by the President, which is still the case with the 1995 constitution. Sir Edward Mutesa's position was not only curious but ambivalent. He was both the KABAKA OF BUGANDA and THE PRESIDENT of UGANDA. Few expected him to give consent to the Referendum (Buyaga and Bugangaizi) Act of 1964. Here was a typical example of conflict of interest . There was no way the Kabaka of Buganda could sign away part of the "territory of his kingdom" and yet the legal requirements of the constitution had to be fulfilled. It was incumbent upon the Clerk to the National assembly to ascertain whether or not the President would attach his signature. The arduous task of submitting the Assent copies of the Act fell on the author who was then the officer in charge of that schedule of duty. He also happened to be a son of the soil of Bunyoro Kitara Kingdom, which was claiming the counties of Buyaga and Bugangaizi- an unenviable situation. The author had on previous occasions performed this duty with ease devoid of any apprehension. However, on this occasion he did not feel comfortable because the political climate was tense and charged with a looming sense of insecurity.

Eventually, I found myself face to face with the President. The venue was the presidential lodge at Makindye in the suburbs of Kampala. When I drove into the compound of the lodge, I could barely see anybody around. The place was quiet, but suddenly an officer appeared on the scene and directed me to an outside shelter where I found His Excellency, the President dressed in army uniform. He was alone. After the preliminary courtesies, I proceeded to present three copies of the Assent Act.

True to the Kiganda tradition, he did not offer me a seat, but since I was there on the service of the government of Uganda I decided to ignore the tradition and pulled a chair. I waited quietly for his reaction- after some time the response came, "these are difficult days, I have to consult one or two persons". That was the last time I spoke to Sir Edward Mutesa II in his capacity as President of Uganda. In the end the Prime Minister signed the Assent copies of the Act. In anticipation that Sir Edward Mutesa would decline to sign the Assent copies of the Bill, legal steps had been taken to enable the Prime Minister to do so. Apparently Sir, Edward Mutesa II was aware of that arrangement. The immediate effect of the passing of the Act was a total collapse of the KY-UPC alliance. From that time onward relations between the two organisations deteriorated by the day.

Most people had foreseen the incongurence between the outward looking Uganda Peoples Congress and the insular Kabaka Yekka group. It is generally believed that the leadership of the Kabaka Yekka hoped to wreck the Uganda Peoples Congress leadership from within the alliance. When that failed the leaders resorted to other measures which were not necessarily constitutional in form or character.

The idea of forming another alliance with the Democratic Party was considered but was found impracticable. The leadership of the two parties had engaged in such acrimonious war of words shortly after the 1962 elections that nothing could repair the damage well enough to establish a good working relationship. Accordingly, that idea was discounted. Meanwhile, the gap between the Central Government and Buganda administration widened. The chances of reconciliation evaporated into thin air. Buganda as a political unit, had to explore other avenues to revive her past glory and maintain her dominant position at the centre stage. Buganda's next posture was a direct result of the frustration arising from the referendum defeat. The power struggle at the centre became real. The internal squabbles within the ruling party assumed a new dimension. Grace Ibingira, Minister of State, who was also the Secretary- General of the party, had by then expanded his political base. With the break up of the KY/UPC alliance, he adopted the strategy of opposing the Prime Minister from within. A significant number of influential Kabaka Yekka members of parliament threw in their lot with the powerful Secretary-General. Some members of Kabaka Yekka remained on government side while others crossed to the opposition benches. It never occurred to any of them to resign as a matter of principle, except one Briton, J.T. Simpson who was minister of economic development. The inference is clear. For the majority of KY members it was a question of marking time in the hope that the office of the Prime Minister might change hands and the alliance revived.

Following the resolution of Parliament passed on August25, 1964, the referendum took place in the counties of Buyaga and Bugangaizi on November 4, 1964. As predicted, the majority of inhabitants of the two counties voted overwhelmingly for return to the jurisdiction of the Bunyoro Kingdom. Thereafter, events in Buganda took a different turn. The balance of power in the Central Government of Uganda became precarious. The population in Buganda became agitated and blamed the referendum defeat and loss of Bugangaizi and Buyaga on the Mengo administration headed by Michael Kintu (the Katikiro/Prime Minister).

A huge demonstration was organised. The demonstrators stormed the Bulange (Buganda council building). At the Bulange the mob threatened to lynch Kintu (the Prime Minister) and attempted to hand in a petition at the Lubiri asking the Kabaka to dismiss the Kintu government. The magnitude of the demonstration was so big that the Central Government Police Force had to intervene to restore law and order. The Katikiro was rescued by the Central Government police from being lynched by the angry mob.

In order to bring the situation under control, riot police were engaged and in the process one school boy was killed by a stray bullet and one police officer was injured. Not long after the eruption of violence in Mengo, another riot took place at Nakulabye, one of Kampala's sprawling suburbs, on November 10, 1964. The shooting started at seven o'clock in the evening and stopped at 10 p. m. How exactly the incident started has remained a matter of conjecture. But the fact is the Nakulabye incident as it came to be popularly known provoked and generated a long acrimonious public debate. For members of parliament on the Opposition benches, it created an opportunity for indicting the Government of Uganda for failure to maintain law and order. On November 10, 1964, Daudi Ochieng, member for Mityana moved the following motion in parliament.

"That this House regrets the shooting of innocent citizens by men of the Security Forces at Nakulabye On November 10, 1964 and conveys its condolences and sympathies to the bereaved and those who suffered in any way. And in view of the fact that government has taken no action, this House calls upon the Government to institute a commission of inquiry headed by a High Court Judge to inquire into this unhappy event and make recommendations." [34]

During the debate it was argued that government had taken no action to alleviate the suffering of the people in the area and expressed the view that the Security Forces had totally failed to handle the situation. It was pointed out that it was not necessary to use excessive force that resulted in the death of four people. The most important point raised was that no government representative visited the scene of the incident to show government concern. It, however, transpired that government had already

[34]   Parliamentary debates (Hasnard) 2nd series Volumes39(pp755-789), 40 9pp866-959; 970-1025):

appointed a coroner to look into the circumstance under which the victims met their death. The coroner had not yet completed his investigations. The coroner's report issued later did not help the situation because the police were blamed for having used excessive force.

The minister responsible for Internal Affairs naturally defended the police saying that the first contingent to arrive at Nakulabye was outnumbered and overwhelmed by a hostile crowd. He alleged that the mover of the motion together with a group of prominent Kabaka Yekka members were capitalising on the incident to advance their own political interests. The inference was that following the Mengo riots, the Katikiro Michael Kintu was left with no alternative but to resign. So, the members in question had their eyes not only on the vacant post of Katikiro but entertained the idea of forming a new government in Mengo. At the end of the debate the House was divided and the motion was defeated by 31 votes against 12 votes. The Nakulabye motion and the debate thereon were forerunners of what was in store for government from Opposition members and others who believed that it was time for change.

The year 1965 must have been one of the most difficult periods for the Prime Minister for his political opponents, both from within his own party and the official parliamentary opposition, were set on bringing his leadership to an end. At first the idea was to get rid of him through constitutional means, preferably by precipitating a crisis that could lead to Parliament passing a motion of no confidence in the government. Mutesa has this to say:

> "Members of the Kabaka Yekka in the National assembly were crossing in dribs and drabs to UPC, lured by the chance of office, the frustration of being an opposition who were not permitted to oppose and not least by Obote's personal powers of persuasion. Some thought they were strengthening the moderate wing that would soon tame, or if necessary dispense with Obote. "[35]

By October 1965, the rupture between the President and the Prime Minister was almost complete. Throughout the independence celebrations, the situation was extremely tense. The Prime Minister made a pregnant address to the nation at the Kololo airstrip where the main celebrations took place. He expressed fears that the country was drifting back into feudalism and strongly condemned agents of neo-colonialism. The then

35   Sir Edward Mutesa, *The Descration of my Kingdom.* (London: Constable 1967)

President, Sir Edward Mutesa acknowledges this fact. "By now, the Prime Minister and I made no pretence of friendship." [36] The little pretence that had existed evaporated into thin air when Mutesa's request to have the Uganda Government Police Band play at his palace in Mengo on the occasion of his birthday was not granted. That was the political atmosphere by the end of 1965.

If there was any place that offered key players in the orchestration of the events that led to the political crisis of 1966, it was the chamber of the National Assembly. There were many actors involved. But Daudi Ochieng stands out as the most vocal and resourceful in this regard. Daudi Ochieng had an edge over his Kabaka Yekka colleagues in the field of parliamentary procedures and legislative matters. He had served as a member of the legislative council before independence when he was appointed Deputy Minister of Finance in November 1960. He was sworn in on November 7 of that year and made his maiden speech on January 30, 1961. His performance was not impressive for a number of reasons. In the first instance, he did not observe known parliamentary niceties, which preclude a new member from introducing controversial issues in his/her maiden speech. In his case there was no way he could have avoided being controversial because the subject he was obliged to introduce related to public funds being diverted from the original purpose for which they were made available. In the second place, in his opening remarks he sneered at the Representative Members who were gunning for the elections slated to take place early that year.

The resolution was as follows: "Be it resolved that the cotton and hard coffee fund be closed as at 1ˢᵗ July 1960, and its assets be transferred to the Capital Development Fund". [37] In the course of introducing the resolution he said, "I am aware that there will be some disappointments among members on the other side of the House who will be standing for election, because it is a straightforward resolution, it is a formality and I know they would have liked something upon which to bite and open their lungs and sort of electioneer on the floor so to speak...." That statement sparked off a swift and angry rebuttal.

Members on the Representative Side retorted that they were in the Council to do a specific job with which they were charged for the benefit of the people of Uganda. The Representative members pointed out that

36   *The Descration of my Kingdom* (London: Contable 1967).
37   *Proceedings Of The Legislative Council Official Report, Part 1; 5ᵗʰ meeting of the 40ᵗʰ session, 30ᵗʰ January 1961*, pp 2082-2092.

the amount of money involved initially came from the "toil and sweat of the peasants" of the country. The money ought to be given to the farmers through the Price Assistance Fund and not to government. Mrs Barbara Saben, MBE, on behalf of the Representatives moved an amendment to that effect. Eventually the debate on the motion (reproduced above), was postponed at the request of the Attorney General. That was not an impressive start for the new Deputy Minister. However, on the personal level what amused the council was that the Deputy Minister had a problem reading out in words the figure of £1,250,000 that represented the first amount voted for in the resolution of 1948. It was an embarrassment to the Front Bench, which consisted of colonial administrators and a few hand picked Africans. From then on Daudi Ochieng picked the rules of the game. He was to use that knowledge extensively in the pursuit of his political goals and in the advancement of KY objectives. He proved a thorn in the flesh of his political opponents.

Daudi Ochieng, described by Sir Edward Mutesa as a "huge boisterous man", is widely remembered for the motion he moved in the National Assembly in 1966, in which he alleged that Colonel Idi Amin and three other persons had acquired large sums of money from gold and ivory looted from the Congo. The three other persons accused were the Prime Minister, Dr A. M. Obote, the Minister of State for Defence Felix Onama, and Adoko Nekyon, Minister of Planning and Economic Development.

He released the information about the matter in doses. The first dose came on March 16, 1965. Four days earlier, V.K Rwamwaro Member of Parliament for Toro East had moved a motion regarding the security situation in Buganda. The full text of the motion read as follows: "Resolved that this House do note with deep regret the rapidly deteriorating security situation in Buganda and urge government to take all necessary measures to ensure security to life and property".[38] Following the collapse of the UPC/KY alliance, the political environment in Buganda became fluid. Uganda Peoples Congress activists started mobilising the population to join the party so as to gain support in Buganda. They embarked on a recruitment campaign and started opening party branches. The Buganda government, which was overwhelmingly Kabaka Yekka, did not take that kindly. Instructions from Mengo to the chiefs throughout the kingdom were that activities of the Uganda Peoples Congress should not be facilitated. The result was intimidation, harassment and even murder became the order of

38   *Parliamentary Debates (Hansard) 2nd Series Volumes 43 and 44,* pp1383-1413; 1453-1493; 1529-1568; 1609-1653; 1706-1737.

the day. It was in the light of these developments that it was decided to take stock of the situation. Parliament once again offered the best forum for that purpose. It must be emphasised that the scope of debate was limited by the terms of the original motion to the region of Buganda. Technically, it would not have been possible for the Opposition to talk about security outside Buganda.

In order to be able to widen the scope of the debate to cover the whole of Uganda, the Opposition proposed a simple amendment to V.K Rwamwaro's motion. The Opposition simply moved that the word "Buganda" be deleted and the word "Uganda" be substituted. That is how Daudi Ochieng managed to raise the question of the alleged gold and ivory obtained from the Congo by Col. Idi Amin. He submitted that there were rumours that some of the army commanding officers were making financial gain out of the Congo and Uganda border military incidents. Paidha and Goli border posts had been bombed by Tshombe's soldiers. A brief account of the political conditions prevailing in the Congo at that time is given later as background information. In short he told the House that the Deputy Commander of the Uganda Armed Forces - Colonel Idi Amin got illegal access to ivory and gold equivalent to Shs. 340,000. He added that the Colonel had opened a bank account with Ottoman Bank and deposited that amount of money between the period February 5 and February 26, 1965. Needless to say, the House was stunned by the allegations. The Minister of Internal Affairs and also responsible for the army F.K. Onama undertook to investigate the allegations. But that was after he had challenged Daudi Ochieng to produce evidence. The only purported evidence produced was a photostat copy of the Bank account deposits. Daudi Ochieng was not done yet. About six months later he bounced back on the floor of the House with greater gusto.

It can be surmised that the onslaught against Idi Amin was to get him out of the way so that the anti-Obote cabinet group led by Grace Ibingira could take over leadership with ease. Ibingira's group had Brigadier Shaban Opolot, Commander of the Army on their side. Background information on the Congo that might help to appreciate the complex political problems that beset the Congo shortly after independence and how Uganda came to be involved in the Congo conflict is given in the next chapter.

Chapter Twelve

The Pigeonhole Constitution And The Ever Recurring Congo

THE GOLD AFFAIR

History has a way of repeating itself. Congo (Leopoldville) currently known as the Democratic Republic of Congo again assumed a new dimension in the politics of Uganda following Lt. General Museveni's military adventure in 1998. Ugandans have never stopped counting their losses in terms of human life, economic and financial costs not to mention the irreparable damage inflicted on Uganda's image in the international community. It is fair to give a brief recent history of Congo's political development especially for the young generation. The Congo achieved independence in June 1960 after seventy years of the worst colonial rule ever experienced on the continent of Africa. Belgium, the colonial power was one of the poorest nations of Europe at that time.

The collapse of colonial rule and the departure of Belgium from the Congo were extremely swift. No major preparations were made to hand over power to the indigenous Congolese before Belgium's exit. The colonial administration was built on three pillars:

i) A bureaucracy consisting of thousands of Belgian civil servants.

ii) A web of international corporations engaged in the exploitation of the country's vast mineral resources as was the case elsewhere in Africa.

iii) A comprehensive structure of religious missions.

Belgium took no heed of the speech of the British Prime Minister, Macmillan that the winds of change were sweeping across the African continent. No political activity by the Congolese was permitted. Despite the ban, a few politically conscious Congolese calling themselves freedom fighters started talking about independence and sensitising their population. Joseph Kasavubu was one such pioneer in the mobilisation of the population. The impact was tremendous. Matters came to a head in 1959 when serious anti-colonial disturbances took place right in the heart of the colony's capital, Leopoldville. Since that time the Congolese never looked back. Belgian Congo became ungovernable. Accordingly, a hastily convened Round Table conference was held in Brussels. Among those who attended the conference were Joseph Kasavubu, Moise Tshombe and a young firebrand by the name of Patrice Lumumba. The independence time-frame was short and the political programme compact. Legislative elections took place in May 1960. The elections began on May 11 and ended on 22. They were marred by violence in the Kasai Province where there were clashes between Baluba and Lulua tribesmen. Leopoldville itself was placed under military rule following a declaration of a state of emergency so as to prevent the fighting from engulfing the capital. No single party emerged with an overall majority in the 137-seat National Assembly. Patrice Lumumba's Movement, *Nationale Congolais* (MNC) and its allies managed to win 41 seats. The National Congress Party and its allies led by Paul Bolya got 12, while the African Solidarity Party of Antoine Gizenga obtained 13, and Joseph Kasavubu's Abakongo Party secured 12.

After hard bargaining, Patrice Lumumba was able to rally the support and approval of 74 representatives out of the total of 137. He was then called upon by the Belgian administration to form a coalition government. The price was to put forward the name of Kasavubu for appointment to the office of President and offer three cabinet posts to the Bakongo Party.

These were the first elections ever held in the country. A new government formed by the Congolese was established on June 24, 1960 with Joseph Kasavubu as President and Patrice Lumumba assumed the office of Prime Minister. A week later it was all over for the Belgian colonialists. The Congo was free. Prime Minister Patrice Lumumba delivered a pregnant speech on the occasion of independence. He reminded men and women of the Congo "about their struggle involving what he called tears, fire and blood, something of which they should be proud of in their deepest hearts. It was a noble and just struggle, which was necessary to bring to an end the humiliating slavery imposed on them by force." He concluded by saying: "We have experienced contempt, insults and blows, morning, noon and night because we are blacks. We shall never forget that a black was called *"tu"* not because he was a friend, but because only the whites were given the honour of being called *"vous"*. He indeed had said all there was to say about the experience of the majority of the Congolese people under Belgian rule.

The end of colonial rule also marked the beginning of Congo's troubles that have bedevilled that African country for the last four decades. The so-called treaty of friendship between Belgium and independent Congo was not even given a chance to operate. Under the treaty the vast majority of the Belgian administrators and technical personnel were to remain at their posts after independence. Evidently, the most critical question was the maintenance of law and order. Independent Congo had no army of her own. However, there were about 25,000 men in uniform known as the Force Publique. The only snag was that the officers were exclusively Belgian. Five days after independence the 25,000 strong Force Publique mutinied against its Belgian officers. Measures taken by the government to meet the soldiers' grievances which included dismissing all Belgian officers and a general promotion of one rank for all men did nothing to restore discipline among the troops. Law and order broke down. The incidence of indiscriminate attack of the white population increased day by day, leading to the white settlers' exodus. Uganda played host to thousands of fleeing Belgians. At the political level relations between President Joseph Kasavubu and Prime Minister Patrice Lumumba were strained. The strain between the top men set in motion a struggle for individual power immediately after the declaration of independence. The situation was exacerbated by the fact that the political leaders at that time lacked a sense of national consciousness. Patrice Lumumba was the exception because he attached "more importance to national unity than to local and tribal interests and thus had a real national following".[39]

Brian Urquhart says his colleagues owed their allegiance to their tribal affiliations hence the proclamation of secession of Katanga by Moise Tshombe on July 11, 1960. Soon after the mutiny Moise Tshombe, Premier of Katanga Province, a mineral rich region providing about 60% of national revenue, announced secession and declared the Province independent. He had the backing of the Belgians and was able to maintain a semblance of law and order in his domain. He eventually gave up secession on August

---

39   Brian Urquhart *Hammarskjold* (Alfred A. Fnopf, New York, 1972) p475.

12 under international pressure at the prompting of the United Nations Secretary General. Meanwhile, Congolese soldiers were busy staging mutiny after mutiny in the rest of the country. Chaos became the order of the day. Law and order broke down completely. It took the intervention of foreign troops under the auspices of the United Nations Organisation to restore a semblance of sanity. The process of restoring law and order proved costly. The Congo became a battlefield for the Cold War. The Western powers led by the United States, France, Britain and Belgium supported factions opposed to Prime Minister Lumumba. He was in turn supported by the Eastern Bloc led by the Union of Soviet Socialist Republics (USSR). "Soviet" was the primary unit of government in Russia and the word means council or committee. (Remember the resistance councils under the National Resistance Movement in Uganda?). Prime Minister Lumumba also enjoyed great support of the few independent African states at that time notably Ghana under Kwame Nkurumah. In addition, Member States of the Afro Asian Committee and the Non-aligned Countries gave his government every possible assistance. Nevertheless, in the final analysis the critical issue was over the control of Congo's vast mineral wealth of gold, diamond, uranium, copper, tin, radium, zinc, cobalt, coal, iron, bauxite, timber and coffee. There was virtually no Central/Federal Government between September 5, 1960 and August 1961. It was during that period that Congo's first Prime Minister, Patrice Lumumba was murdered in Katanga on January 17, 1961 on the orders of Colonel Mobutu who was then Chief of Staff of the army in collusion with Moise Tshombe and his Belgian collaborators. Little more than five years later, his tormentor and murderer Mobutu, overwhelmed by the high accolade bestowed on Lumumba by the Continent of Africa and the non-aligned countries of Asia succumbed to the pressure and lamely proclaimed Lumumba a national hero. This is what he said, "On this historical day, June 30, 1966 when our country is taking its first steps towards winning economic independence, how can we fail to recall that great figure, Patrice Lumumba, for great he was and great he will remain. In the name of the government we ask you to keep silent for a minute in memory of the man we proclaim officially today a national hero Patrice Emery Lumumba."

The following excerpt from the United Nations Secretary General's address to the Council delivered on February 15, 1961 lends credence to the above assessment of the Congo situation. "For seven or eight months, through efforts far beyond the imagination of those who founded this organisation, it has tried to counter tendencies to introduce the *big power conflict* into Africa and put the Young African countries *under the shadow of the cold war.* It has done so with great risks and against heavy odds. It has done so at the cost of very great personal sacrifices for a great number of people….We countered effectively efforts from all **sides** *to make the Congo a happy hunting ground for their national interests.* To be a road block to such efforts is to make yourselves the target of attacks *from all those* who find their plans thwarted".[40] In an effort to end the secession of Katanga, Hammarskjold agreed to meet Tshombe in neighbouring Northern Rhodesia. While on his way to the agreed venue, the Secretary General died in a plane crash under suspicious circumstances, on September 17, 1961 near Ndola in present day Zambia. Zambia was then known as Northern Rhodesia. It had strong links with apartheid South Africa. Both countries supported Moise Tshombe. After the Hammarskjold tragedy, every effort by the United Nations was made to end the Katanga secession. Eventually, Katanga returned to the fold in January 1963.

One and half years later, the United Nations Force withdrew from the Congo. An uneasy peace prevailed and a month later, Moise Tshombe became Prime Minister. He was in turn faced with a rebellion in Kwilu and Eastern Congo led by Pierre Mulele Gizenga and Gbenye, staunch supporters of Patrice Lumumba. The struggle for power intensified after the second coup by General Mobutu against Moise Tshombe. Thousands joined the armed struggle. Towns fell, one after another. It was that struggle spearheaded by the Congolese Revolutionary Movement against the reactionaries in Kinshasa that drew Uganda into the conflict across the border in West Nile.

The civil war in Congo had a direct impact on Uganda. There was a continuous influx of refugees which raised serious concern about insecurity at the border, especially in the West Nile region. In order to contain the situation, the Uganda government set up a committee in November 1964 to deal with the dual problem of the influx of refugees from the Congo and the maintenance of the security of Uganda. By the end of the year the government was prompted to assist the regime of Gbenye, following the Stanleyville (now Kisangani) incident when Belgian paratroopers stormed the place allegedly to rescue Belgian citizens. It was due to that commitment that a high ranking military officer was detailed to take charge of the military assistance Uganda was to provide to the Gbenye regime.

40   Brian Urquhart *Haammarskjold,* (Alfred A. Knopf, New York, 1972) pp.507-8.

Meanwhile, the presidents of Kenya and Tanzania together with Gbenye leading a delegation of the Congolese Revolutionary Movement, converged in Mbale on January 13, 1965 to endorse the Ugandan government's commitment to military assistance to the Gbenye regime. Uganda Prime Minister A.M. Obote played host to the meeting. The military officer to co-ordinate the assistance was none other than the second in command of the Ugandan army, Colonel Idi Amin. The nature of assistance and other activities connected therewith were for obvious reasons not made public. Daudi Ochieng's curiosity prompted him to find out what was happening. This partly explains the discrepancies in his submissions made to Parliament. He ignored the fact that transparency and accountability did not come easily in the realm of post-independence revolutionary governments. To be sure, Parliament deserved more information than the government was prepared to give.

To return to the gathering of the political storm in Uganda, Daudi Ochieng having waited in vain for over five months for government to act on the allegations against Amin raised in the House in March of that year decided to reactivate the issue. He submitted a parliamentary question No.441 of 1965 regarding the banking of monies by Amin belonging to the Congolese Revolutionary Movement. He quoted a cable sent to him by one Olenga Nicholas who passed as General in the circles of the revolutionary movement. In response government gave a long written reply denying responsibility for private bank accounts in possession of foreigners. The opposition did not consider the reply satisfactory. So, the questioner decided to proceed with the issue in a more substantive form. On September 7, an oral notice of motion was given to that effect. Nine days later the following motion standing in the name of Daudi Ochieng was moved in the House: "With a view to clear (sic.) his name, this House do request government to appoint a commission to enquire into the allegations contained in the cable from General Olenga Nicholas, that Idi Amin is involved in the banking of moneys belonging to the Congolese rebels".[41]

The House was set for the most acrimonious debate in the history of Independent Uganda and the government thought it wise in the national interest for the deliberations to be conducted in camera. The deputy Minister of Education and Government Chief Whip, Shaban Nkutu proposed a formal motion, "That strangers do move from the Public Gallery'. The Galleries were cleared of all members of the public.

41   *Parliamentary Debates (Hansard) Second Series Volume 52, p3159.*

The debate proceeded but no record was made. It was however agreed that an amicable solution would be found. Government disclosed that investigations were nearing completion. Apparently, nothing of the sort happened in the intervening period thus precipitating the last onslaught by the indomitable Daudi Ochieng. He then tabled a resolution demanding the suspension of Colonel Idi Amin from duty. The investigations referred to in the Secret Session were not Police investigations but mere enquiries at cabinet level.

The resolution read as follows: "That this House do urge government to suspend from duty Colonel Idi Amin pending the conclusion of police investigations into the allegations regarding his bank account, which should then be passed on to the appropriate authority whose final decision on the matter shall be made public". [42] In his presentation Ochieng told the House that the Colonel was engaged in training dissidents in Mbale whose aim was to overthrow the government of Uganda. That was not all. He further claimed that the Prime Minister Dr. Apollo Milton Obote, the Minister of Defence Felix Onama, and the Minister of Planning and Economic Development A.A Nekyon were involved in the gold and ivory affair. He went on to say that the Prime Minister had received an equivalent of £50,000 while each of the two ministers had received half of that amount. Those were preposterous allegations made against the head of government and his two close cabinet ministers. The House was subdued. None of the cabinet ministers raised a finger in protest and the motion was almost unanimously adopted. The only dissenting voice came from John Kakonge who in his contribution suggested an amendment to call for the resignation of the government. (He did not formally move the proposed amendment) He complained that some ministers knew of the new disclosures and took no action. For others, he surmised, it was Amin standing in their way so he must be removed to clear the way. The Speaker adjourned the House sine die at 9.45 p.m. in an atmosphere of anxiety fraught with danger and political uncertainty.

The motion was designed to raise doubts about the credibility of the government of the day and to bring Obote's leadership into disrepute. However, the resolution fell short of the vote of no confidence. Albeit, it brought about confusion within the ranks of the government.

The confusion arose out of the fact that the Government Parliamentary Group at the meeting held on January 31, 1966 had after a long discussion, decided to reject Daudi Ochieng's motion. It is also a fact that members of the cabinet had had occasion to discuss the matter three times since the issue was first raised in parliament. They were also aware of the fact that efforts to set up a Board of Inquiry manned by military officers were abandoned due to legal difficulties. What compounded the issue was the fact that the cabinet on the day the motion was moved decided to reverse the decision taken earlier by the Parliamentary Group. None of the cabinet ministers offered an explanation to the backbenchers for the change of heart. Was there a sinister conspiracy?

Rumours of an impending coup freely circulated around town. Big sums of money changed hands, suspicion and mistrust were the order of the day. It was frightening. It was at the same time an occasion that proved to be a source of amusement to see petty minds of politicians at work from close quarters. For example, when the motion on the gold allegations was moved and debated, the Prime Minister was out of town. He was on tour in Northern Uganda. It was imperative that both the Prime Minister and the President should be apprised of National Assembly deliberations on the motion. As Chief Executive of the National Assembly staff, I was under obligation to let the Prime Minister have a transcript of the proceedings of that particular sitting as soon as it was humanly possible. Accordingly, instructions were issued to the entire staff especially the audio-typists, not to sign off when the House adjourned. A verbatim recording of the proceedings had to be produced before daybreak. That was done. The staff went home in the small hours of the morning. A transcript copy of the proceedings was immediately dispatched to the Prime Minister as previously arranged. Another copy was personally delivered to the President at Makindye Lodge, which was within walking distance from the Speaker's official residence. That was what efficiency was all about. The politicians with petty minds thought otherwise. The group opposed to the Prime Minister blamed me personally for delivering the proceedings to the embattled Prime Minister so promptly. The other group saw no reason why the President, in addition to the transcript, was given access to the actual tape record of the proceedings. That was the highest exhibition of petty mindedness on the part of the misguided politicians. It is unfortunate that type of behaviour subsists up to the present day. There is no question about accepting a given administrative system or looking at a given issue objectively. For the petty-minded politicians, politics must revolve around personality, intrigue and intimidation. One must not stand by the rules of the game. In the words of Dan Mudoola, "The subsequent years up to 1966 were characterised by groups seeking maximum benefits out of the constitutional arrangements. Groups were only too ready when in a position of strength, not to adhere to them if they did not serve their interests." [43] More often than not, National Assembly staff had to contend with that dilemma. The staff closed their ears and stood their ground.

It was on this basis that I was able to continue much to the discomfort of the political leadership paying monthly allowances to the five ministers detained in 1966 until the lapse of six months. In this regard the independence constitution of 1962 in spelling out disqualification for membership of the National Assembly, specified that under section 40(d): "No person shall be qualified to be a member of National Assembly who is…or under sentence of imprisonment (by whatever name called) exceeding six months imposed on him by such a court or substituted by competent authority for some other sentence imposed on him by such a court".

Back to the aftermath of Ochieng's motion: the Prime Minister returned to Entebbe on February 13, 1966 and denied the allegations by declaring at a press conference, " This is a frame up to present me as the dirtiest man in Uganda…I have led this country with clean hands and a clean heart" (Uganda Argus, February 14, 1966). By coincidence that was the same day Dr. Emmanuel Lumu defeated Godfrey Binaisa in an election contest for the office of UPC chairman, Buganda Region. The Prime Minister after taking stock of the situation reacted on February 22, 1966 by arresting five cabinet Ministers to contain the situation from getting worse. Most Ugandans were stunned by the turn of events. The manner in which the arrest of the five ministers was effected left much to be desired. A more dignified and humane way of handling men of that stature ought to have been adopted. The five ministers were arrested in the course of a Cabinet meeting and in the full view of other colleagues. The spectacle had a very demoralising effect on other ministers. Because no immediate public announcement was made giving details of the arrest and detention there was unnecessary panic in government circles and among spouses and relatives of the affected ministers. The decision to restrict the suspects outside Kampala exacerbated matters. It led to negative publicity following the tussle over habeas corpus writ in the High Court. Placing the minister under house arrest in the capital pending investigations would have been a less degrading option and eased the task of damage control. Ugandans must learn to acknowledge and uphold the dignity and trappings attached to key positions in public life. It is not difficult to separate the

43   Dan Mudoola "Religion Ethnicity and Politics" p.25.

mischief of an occupant of a given high office from the standing or status of the office.

The manner of arrest and detention of the five cabinet ministers and subsequent events sent powerful signals that Uganda's experiment in Parliamentary democracy modelled on the Westminster pattern could not stand the test of time. The ministers who were arrested and detained were Grace Ibingira, Minister of State, Dr. Emanuel Lumu, Minister of Health, B.K. Kirya, Minister of Works, G.B.K Magezi, Minister of Labour and M.M. Ngobi, Minister of Agriculture. Ibingira was one of those persons who served as members of legislative council before independence. He came to the Legislative Council as a nominee of the Mugabe of Ankole. At the time he entered Legislative Council he was a promising young lawyer. He looked ambitious, was moderate in his political views and, I daresay, cunning in the scheme of things. He was highly respected by the British administrators who sat in the Council. He got on very well with the non-African Representatives of the Legislative Council presumably because of the moderate views he held.

By the time of independence, he had grown out of sectarian politics based on 'nationality'. He was set for playing a meaningful role in national politics. It was a general belief that if the East African Federation had materialised, he would have assumed the mantle of Prime Minister in Uganda. The failure to form the federation appears to have been one of his frustrations. In the run up to the 1966 crisis he became a central figure around whom party dissidents rallied. His election as Secretary-General in 1964 split the party into two antagonistic factions. His main rival, John Kakonge who enjoyed tremendous support of the Youth League and the Trade Unions, did not share Ibingira's political philosophy. He believed in creating an egalitarian Uganda society or rather a Welfare State. Grace Ibingira, on the other hand, was a staunch believer in capitalism, a sort of a forerunner of Thatcher and Reagan. In his bid to oust Kakonge, Ibingira had solid support of the cabinet and the majority of members of parliament. He also seems to have received tactical approval of the Prime Minister whose sole desire at that material time was to put an end to party factionalism by calling to order the powerful youth league and the militant trade unions. That task could not be tackled effectively so long as John Kakonge remained Secretary-General of the party. Hence, the drastic Trade Union Movement and the Youth reorganisation that followed. But the Obote- Ibingira accord could not and did not last long. The two men had quite different political outlooks. Obote was a republican and preferred a socialistic pattern of society to capitalism without a human face. Grace Ibingira performed well in parliament. He was brilliant, knew his way about in parliamentary procedure. Above all, he had the intellectual capacity to articulate his point of view thus raising the level of debate to an appreciable standard. I have always wondered how he managed to get along with some of his close confidants who were not so gifted.

B.K. Kirya, an ex-serviceman was yet another of those Members of Parliament who served in the Legislative Council before Independence. He had a strong political base in his home district. Largely, a self-made man with good native intelligence and amenable to new ideas, he was capable of being rough and ruthless in pursuit of his political interests. For a long time he was a close associate of Milton Obote until the end of 1963 when he succumbed to external pressures to help remove his mentor. He was a good public relations man and was able to move in Buganda's high social circles in an effort to promote the Party. He had good contact at the highest level in the Lubiri (Kabaka's court) and for that reason he was deeply involved in the formation of the alliance with the Kabaka Yekka. Unlike George Magezi and Grace Ibingira, he did not possess the attributes of a good debater in parliament. A small incident of great interest took place when he was minister of works. He was one of the ministers who showed scant regard for government financial regulations. He made an order to have a booklet printed outside normal government procedures. His accounting officer advised against the printing of the booklet and the proposed expenditure. He insisted and went ahead with the order for the pamphlet. The accounting officer managed to get a written note to the effect that despite the advice of his officials, he would not rescind the order. The degree of financial discipline in the ministries was very high during the first five years of independence. The Auditor General in his report made an adverse comment on the expenditure. He classified it as irregular. In the process of examining the auditors report, the Public Accounts Committee of the National Assembly of which I was Secretary, queried that item of expenditure. The responsible officials of the Ministry were able to prove that they had done all that was expected of them as custodians of public funds in their ministry. They explained they were overruled by the Minister. Accordingly, the Public Accounts Committee recommended that a token amount of money should be recovered from the Minister to signify that parliament took great exception to the Minister's conduct regarding public funds. The amount of money was quite negligible, but the principle was of great importance. That was the state of financial accountability before the "liberators" of the seventies and the late eighties appeared on the scene and "liberated" officials and politicians alike to dig deep into national coffers with little or no hindrance.

G.B.K. Magezi was one of the longest serving parliamentarians in the post-independence administration. He was initially nominated to the Legislative Council by the Rukurato of Bunyoro Kingdom (Bunyoro's mini parliament). With hard work and goodwill from both sides of the Legislative Council, he quickly made his mark on the floor of the Council. In 1958 he returned to the Legislative Council as an elected representative for Bunyoro to join other elected African representatives from nine Districts. The African elected members formed an organisation of their own that became extremely vocal. Aware of the fact that independence was in sight and having regard for the internal squabbles within the Uganda National Congress, he joined the non-Congress elected members, mainly from the Western region to found the Uganda Peoples Union. Following the appointment of the Wild Committee of which he was a member, the UPU and the Obote-Mayanja faction of UNC successfully worked out a merger to form and launch a new Party-the Uganda Peoples Congress. George Magezi was appointed General-Secretary of the new Party. The appointment propelled him into the main stream of national politics. He played a very active part in Parliament, especially during the period UPC was in opposition. He and his colleagues on the Opposition Benches made life difficult for the DP government. I remember him as an ardent advocate of Protestant chauvinism and also a great admirer of the western way of life, especially the British way of life. He was not inclined towards socialism or communism. Few could distinguish between the two in a scientific analysis. From 1955 to 1962 he enjoyed tremendous support from his supporters in Bunyoro. The alliance between UPC and KY estranged him from his constituents of South Bunyoro. His involvement in the alliance cost him his seat in the elections of April 1962. His devout Catholic colleague, John Babiiha from Toro, suffered the same fate. Since the two were influential members of the Uganda Peoples Congress, they were able to get into Parliament as specially elected members. I doubt whether Magezi ever forgave his constituents for the embarrassment and the humiliation he went through. In terms of practical politics there is a great contrast between what happened to him in 1962 and what happened to Milton Obote after the introduction of the Common Man's Charter. Both men believed they were acting in the best interests of their people. Both of them faltered in their communication to the people expected to benefit from the objectives they set out to achieve. George Magezi was concerned with what he believed was a larger issue of achieving independence for Uganda and gaining power for his Political Party. He failed totally to carry that message to the people he represented. To do so would have required a sizeable number of his political agents in Hoima to be convinced of the merits of the Party's strategy and goals. Unfortunately, tribal feelings outstripped political Party affiliation. By and large, local party loyalty revolved around some personality. In this case George Magezi symbolised the Party in Bunyoro. He could not, single-handed, sell the party strategy to his constituents.

That has been the tragedy of political party organisation in this country. Party organisation has always been run from top to bottom. No structures have ever been in place to filter and channel Political Party strategies and policies to the grass roots. The common man's charter, under the authorship of Milton Obote met the same fate. Dr, Milton Obote had neither the machinery nor personnel sufficiently committed to disseminate the new ideology to the population. That is why the new ideology ended in a fiasco.

That Magezi joined the dissident group of cabinet ministers against his long time political associate, Dr. Milton Obote, took many observers by surprise. Insiders argue that he was recruited at the very last moment and that matters of ideology must have played a decisive role in his decision. He must have been persuaded to join the group so as to fight communism-that monster and enemy of civilised societies. Did ethnicity play a part in the conspiracy?

Dr. Lumu came to Parliament on a KY ticket. After the collapse of the alliance he gravitated towards UPC. He is known to have been an ultra-traditionalist who presumably joined the Party with the intention of destroying it from within. On February 13, 1966 he was elected UPC chairman, Buganda Region. The Office of Chairman, Buganda Region, was hotly contested between him and Godfrey Binaisa. Binaisa was pro-Obote at the time. Dr Lumu's victory was a morale booster for the dissident group. It was all part of the scheme to demoralise the Prime Minister and to prepare the way for a final push. It was a false hope.

Earlier in the 1950s Dr Lumu was one of the ultra-traditionalists from Buganda who would not stand to see the construction of Parliamentary Building in Kampala the eventual home of Uganda's Parliament in the Capital City. The group held the view that the location of Parliament House in Kampala to cater for the whole of Uganda would diminish and undermine the status of Bulange, the home of the Lukiko (Buganda mini parliament) at Mengo. That was an extremely myopic view. However, Lumu's membership in the National Assembly seems to have uplifted and widened his vision. He fell in love with national politics and was ready to maintain his position at any cost. He paid dearly. He has since his incarceration kept a low profile and completely withdrawn from public life. The events of 1966 must have come to him as a great surprise and must have shocked him. In parliament I remember him as a soft- spoken man, always well-clad, and often had great difficulty in making himself understood, especially during the hectic Question Time.

After the arrest and detention of the five ministers, Dr Obote announced the suspension of the 1962 Constitution and told the nation that he had assumed all powers of government and declared himself President. In April 1966 he introduced a new constitution which has come to be known as the "pigeon-hole constitution". The effect of the 1966 constitution was to concentrate power in the centre and to reverse the devolution of power to the kingdoms of Buganda, Bunyoro, Toro and Ankole, the Territory of Busoga and the Districts, which had been enshrined in the Independence Constitution. The high office of the President became executive and that of Prime Minister was abolished. The federal and quasi-federal structures in the Kingdoms and the Territory of Busoga were dismantled. Buganda's option to hold indirect elections for National Assembly representatives was scrapped. The kingdoms were highly incensed by these developments. But it was only Buganda that publicly denounced the measures and declared that they were not acceptable. The Buganda government invoked the argument of the social contract theory enunciated centuries ago by Hobbes and Locke, except that the circumstances under which Buganda and the state of Uganda entered into the social contract were quite different from that expounded by the two political philosophers. Nevertheless, the Buganda government postulated that Dr. Milton Obote as an agent of the Uganda government had violated the contract. The Lukiko in order to signify Buganda's disengagement passed a resolution on May 20 1966, calling on the government of Uganda to remove itself from Buganda soil. The Uganda government authorities interpreted the Lukiko resolution as a grave act of rebellion. The next thing was eruption of riots in Buganda. Four days later instructions were issued to deal with the situation at Mengo. The military expedition was led by Idi Amin, Deputy Commander of the Uganda army. Professor K. Ingham asserts that: "A bungled attempt under the military command of Colonel Idi Amin, to seize the person of the Kabaka, resulted in more violence than had been intended. The Kabaka escaped and eventually found refuge in England and the former resentment of the Ganda blossomed into open hatred of Obote's government".[44] That aptly sums up the relationship between Buganda and the Central Government by the middle of 1966. The situation did not improve in the next four years. Buganda was declared a disturbed area and continued to be under state of emergency up to the time of the 1971 coup d'etat. Such state of affairs did not inspire confidence among a substantial number of Baganda who had the courage to defy the general sentiments of their fellow Baganda and were prepared to go along with the rest of Uganda.

The 1966 crisis brought the military to the forefront of the country's body politic. Those in authority came to rely more and more on the military might. On the day the new constitution of 1966 was introduced in the National Assembly, an outside observer standing at a distance from Parliament House, would have rightly mistaken the precincts of Parliament as part of a military post or garrison. Bands of heavily armed soldiers were stationed in the beautiful and well-maintained parliamentary gardens that were used from time to time for cocktail parties and other government functions. Members of Parliament were searched not only at the main entrance of the building but also in the Division Lobbies as they entered the Chamber. Typical of Ugandan politicians none but one member protested against such high handedness in dealing with Honourable Members of Parliament.

It was Shafiq Arain who sought to uphold the dignity of the House by questioning the propriety of soldiers searching Members of Parliament within the precincts of Parliament. Shafiq Arain represented a new breed of young intellectuals who were descendants of Asians from mainly India and Pakistan. More often than not, Asians are credited with contributing to the economic development of the country. But nothing is mentioned about the role the Asian community played in the struggle for independence. Credit ought to be given where it is due. In 1957 a small group of young educated Asians composed of Waheed Karim, Anil Clerk, Pandya, Shafiq Arain, Gurdial Singh, Misri and Panda issued a statement of intent to form the Uganda action group. Dr. M.M. Patel, a distinguished physician was appointed chairman. The statement clearly stated that the Uganda Action Group was 'completely non racial' and that it was not meant to 'consolidate and protect the Asian interests in a changing Uganda'. The

44   *Politics in Modern Uganda: The Uneven Tribal Dimension.* 1990 Routledge, London (P19).

group acknowledged that the colonial administration social legislation tended to favour the two immigrant communities of Europeans and Asians and explained that the preferential treatment accorded to the two communities enabled them to acquire great wealth, political influence and social status in Uganda. The group observed: " the most tragic outcome of this unimaginative pattern of development was the creation of a water tight division between the Africans and non Africans which is liable to stultify even the authentic attempt to mould the peoples of Uganda into a single harmonious unit today."

Accordingly, the group declared that young Asians were determined to play a part as Ugandans in the great political drama, which was to shape their future destiny. They were ready to suffer and make sacrifices for the noble cause, which was the emancipation of Uganda. This was a bold declaration, considering that it was made at a time when the older generation of Asians was campaigning for the entrenchment of the minority rights in independent Uganda.

A policy statement outlining the aims and objectives of the group was issued in April 1959. It proclaimed that the Uganda Action Group had been formed with the object of creating in Uganda, by peaceful and legitimate means, a free and democratic nation based on equality of opportunity and of political, social and economic rights with the aim of attaining universal fellowship and world peace. The task ahead was to educate the immigrant communities to the prevailing realities of the country and to weave a new nation from the complex strands of the various racial and tribal elements that inhabited Uganda.

The Uganda Action Group prophetically asserted that it was proper for the people of Uganda to recognise the fact that they were ONE NATION and that unless the unqualified unity was achieved in all fields of human endeavour Uganda would forever be squandering its limited resources in fratricidal conflicts even after the attainment of independence. The group's main preoccupation was to interact with leaders of a multitude of political parties that had mushroomed with a view to reducing their number to a meaningful and manageable level. Eventually, most of the founder members of the Group joined the Uganda People's Congress. It was on the strength of their UPC membership that both Shafiq Arain and Anil Clerk found their way into the National Assembly as specially elected members. Tribute must be paid to the young pioneers for their foresight and strong belief in the universality of mankind and the inherent equality and dignity of man irrespective of colour, race or religion.

We return to the National Assembly proceedings of April 15, 1966. To add insult to injury, copies of the new constitution were distributed after the day's sitting of Parliament and hence the name "pigeon-hole constitution". It may be argued that such incidents were minor and were necessary in view of the gravity of the political and security situation. To such argument one would ask, what was the efficacy of convening the National Assembly when it was obvious that the situation did not permit discussion or debate? The whole exercise was demoralising. It gave ammunition to government detractors. Above all, it was a negation of democracy. After that incident, the National Assembly was never the same again. Members of Parliament were gripped by fear from which they never recovered. The standing and esteem of Parliament were diminished in the eyes of the security organs. For instance, there was a time when a high-ranking officer of the General Service (intelligence organisation) attempted to banish an Opposition member of Parliament from the Uganda club described in Chapter 14. The official actually pulled out a pistol and pointed it at the Honourable Member in order to enforce the ban. I was called upon to intervene in the matter in my capacity as Secretary of the Management Committee of the club. Such incidents minor as they were marked the beginning of the erosion of civic authority and the ascendancy of militarism in Uganda's body politic. It became difficult to revert to the old order and re-establish the rule of law.

The acceptance by the National Assembly of Daudi Ochieng's motion on February 4, 1966 had serious repercussions on the functioning of the government and its credibility. Damage control measures had to be taken. The first backlash was the detention of the five cabinet ministers believed to have been conspiring to oust Prime Minister Obote from leadership. Then came the suspension of a substantial portion of the 1962 constitution. With Sir Edward Mutesa out of contention and his associates in detention, the Prime Minister moved to the next phase of the cleansing exercise. He set out to clear his name and the image of the government. He resorted to the old age convention to deal with the matter. A commission of inquiry was appointed to look into:

- The allegations of the receipt by Honourable Dr. Apollo Milton Obote, Prime Minister, the Honourable Felix Kenyi Onama, Minister of State for Defence, the Honourable Akbar Akaki Adoko Nekyon, Minister of Planning and Community Development and Colonel Idi Amin Deputy Commander of the Army, of gold, ivory, monies or other property from the

Congo made by the Honourable Daudi Ochieng in the debate on the motion moved by the said Honourable Member on February 4, 1966.

- The allegations of conspiracy, plot or plots to compel by force of arms or constraint or otherwise the nullification, abrogation or defeasance of the constitution, made by Honourable Daudi Ochieng in the said debate.

- Allegations of conspiracy, plot or plots to compel by force of arms or constraint, the intimidation, coercion or the overthrow of government -as by law established in the course of the debate on the said motion moved by the said Honourable Member.

Members of the Commission were:

Mr Justice Sir Clement Nageon de L'Estang

Vice President of the court of appeal for Eastern Africa (Chairman).

Mr Justice Augustine Saidi

Judge of the High Court of the United Republic of Tanzania.

Mr Justice Henry Cecil Ethelwood Miller

Judge of the High Court of the Republic of Kenya

Mr Samuel Wako Wambuzi (Secretary)

The Commission was assisted by:

Mr John Rankin of the English Bar together with Mr Festus Rukunda,

Mr John Wilmers Q C and Achroo Ram Kapila represented Dr A. M Obote, F.K Onama and A.A.A Nekyon,

The Honourable Anil Clerk represented Col Idi Amin,

Mr Wilkinson and Mr Patel represented Daudi Ochieng,

Mr Keeble represented Mr. S.M. Venter of Commercial Bank of Africa,

Mr Gurdial Singh represented Captain Christopher Kisembo

Mr John Kazzora represented the five ministers who were in detention.

The commission sat between March 8 and 25, 1966; heard evidence from ninety- three witnesses. Apparently, only a few of those witnesses were of material assistance to the commission. The ninety odd witnesses included the much 'hyped' Brigadier Olenga Nicholas Philip of whom the commission "formed the impression that he knew nothing of his own knowledge and was quite unwilling to assist the commission for reasons best known to himself".

The commission reported, inter-alia, as follows:

"We find (1) that the allegations of the receipt by the Honourable Prime Minister, the Honourable Felix Onama and the Honourable A. A. A Nekyon of gold ivory, monies and other property from the Congo are totally unsupported by evidence and completely unfounded". In other words, the commission exonerated the Prime minister and the two ministers.

Chapter Thirteen

The Common Man's Charter

The period between April 1966 and October 1969 was perilous. There was a cloud of uncertainty. The country was shocked by the 1966 crisis with all its attendant political implications. Then came the Republican Constitution of September 1967, which abolished kingdoms and established a unitary form of government with the concentration of power in the presidency. Pluralism and the political philosophy of unity in diversity virtually came to an end. There was apathy and the vibrant political activities of the immediate post-independence era were no more. The militant Youth League had its wings clipped though the Trade Unions proved a hard nut to crack. The trend towards centralisation did not stop at government level. Centralisation also engulfed the ruling political party structure.

The main feature of the UPC new constitution adopted in June 1968 was centralisation. The Party President was empowered to nominate the Executive committee thus relegating the notion of elective office and internal democracy to history books. The NRM adopted a similar system in the Movement Act thereby constitutionalising the Movement. The fundamental change is yet to come. To wind up the experiment on parliamentary democracy, members of the Opposition started crossing to Government benches in great numbers. One should remember that the one-party state system was in vogue in Africa. African leaders believed that the *One-Party State System* was 'home-grown'. Nobody dared to tell the uninformed or ill-informed African masses that the system was the greatest import from Russia and China.

By the end of 1969 Dr. Milton Obote had consolidated his position and emerged as national leader despite the political hiccup in Buganda. He then felt it was time Uganda developed an ideology she would call her own. Tanzania had, it was believed, evolved the ideology of Ujamaa, Kaunda's Zambia had developed the philosophy of Humanism. Kenya was smarting under the banner of African Socialism. Those were high sounding political doctrines. The Move to the Left was presented to the world as Uganda's contribution to the African revolution. To amplify what the Move to the Left was all about, five ideological documents were produced detailing the essential aspects of the new political culture. The Common Man's Charter (October 1969) was document No. 01. It laid down broad outlines of the new ideology. The document highlighted impediments to Uganda's political and economic development such as capitalism, feudalism, foreign influence, colonial system of education, the landed gentry and privileges based on heredity.

The main theme of the document was the need to arouse nationalism and create socialism, which would revolutionise the Ugandan society. Paragraph II of the Charter proclaimed: "The Move to the Left is the creation of a new political chapter and a new way of life, whereby the people of Uganda as a whole, their welfare and their voice in the National government and in their local authorities, were paramount. It was, therefore, both anti-feudalism and anti-capitalism". Document No. 02 contained proposals for National Service. The threshhold for the National Service was rural development so as to improve rural life and stem the migration of the rural population to urban areas. It was also designed to encourage self-reliance. The proposed national camps were meant to bring about greater interaction among different people drawn from different parts of the country. A new ministry, the Ministry of National Service, was created to take charge of training camps at all levels. The training centres at constituency level were meant to deal with the youth, school leavers including university graduates. The task of nation-building was to be inculcated into the minds of the young Ugandans. The idea was to re-orient the youth towards society, their own community and the country as a whole. The document on National Service evoked a great deal of debate because almost the entire population, except children and the aged, was expected to be involved in the exercise. The idea of national service ought to be revisited. A well organised and adequately funded National Service could one day change the face of Uganda. The target group should be the youth. Every young man or woman in possession of 'O' and 'A' level education who proceeds to university, tertiary institution, or other centre of higher education should "volunteer" to do a national service in the field of his or her academic inclination at the end of the course. Nobody should be awarded a degree, diploma or certficate in whatever field of study before undergoing and completing the national service. Participants would be introduced to Civics, basic military training and then do practical work in one's field of education. Document No. 03 represented a statement made by the President when he addressed the National Assembly on April 20, 1970. The purpose of the document was to provide further clarification on the Move to the Left. Document No. 04 was the most controversial and had far greater impact on the events that followed the launching of the Common Man's Charter. It contained the Presidents Speech delivered on the occasion of Labour Day, which came to be known as the Nakivubo pronouncements. The document was a direct result of article 38 of the Charter, which simply stated: "in our move to the left strategy, we affirm that the guiding economic principle will be that the means of production and distribution must be in the hands of the people as a whole. The fulfilment of this principle may involve nationalisation of the enterprises privately owned". The message was loud and clear. It sent different signals to different groups. Reaction from Britain and United States of America was swift and emphatic. The two countries expressed great concern and declared that the measures contained in the Nakivubo Pronouncements were totally unacceptable. They believed Milton Obote was becoming too independent for their liking. The British and American reaction must be seen in terms of the prevailing cold war at the time. What were the contents of the Nakivubo pronouncements? The government of Uganda was to assume 60% shares in about eighty major industries in the country.

The industries included all oil companies, the Kampala and District Bus Companies, Kilembe Mines, the manufacturing industries, plantations, insurance companies, banking and credit institutions. The government undertook to compensate the owners of the affected industries and companies over a period of fifteen years. The measures took immediate effect. There was outrage in Britain. The BBC dubbed the measures "outright expropriation". These were bold measures, which involved monetary reform, nationalisation and rationalisation of foreign policy.

There was also document No. 05 titled *The Move to the Left Strategy: Proposals for the New Methods of Election of Representatives of the people to Parliament*, which sought to introduce new electoral proposals, namely, one basic constituency plus three national constituencies. It also spelt out proposals for the election of the President of the Republic of Uganda. The latter attracted greater public debate. Unfortunately, the National Council of UPC under the influence of sycophants rejected the proposal for direct election of the President by the masses. The Council recommended that the President of the Party should automatically be the President of the country. That was a deviation from the declared path of democratisation. It was bad politics. It sent out to the nation and the international community a wrong signal. In fact, it was one of the factors that gave ammunition to the opposition groups to wage a campaign against the President and accuse him of dictatorial tendencies. The Democratic Party condemned the decision.

To say that the Move to the Left did not achieve the desired results would be an understatement. We have seen that the power struggle that preceded the 1964 Gulu Annual Party Conference left the Uganda Peoples Congress divided into two factional camps. One of the factions was headed by the victorious Grace Ibingira who emerged from the conference as Secretary-General. John Kakonge headed the other faction with the backing of the Youth League and the Trade Unions. The Party President at that time sided with the moderates viz. the Ibingira group. In the intervening period between 1964 and 1966 a drift developed between Ibingira and Obote. By 1966 relations between the new Secretary-General and the President were strained to breaking point. The estrangement between Milton Obote and Grace Ibingira led to the 1966 crisis and the latter's arrest and detention together with four other cabinet ministers. By the time the Move to the left was launched, the UPC, as James Mittleman puts it "was moribund and President Obote would not even trust senior officials. Local notables continued to dominate the country and rural branches were frequently at odds with Central Headquarters in Kampala. The party did not penetrate to the grass roots". [45]

After John Kakonge's ouster, the normal party machinery broke down. The centre of activities shifted from headquarters to Parliament where UPC members of Parliament were the party's leaders in their respective constituencies. The parliamentary constituencies served as party organs headed by the sitting members of parliament. This created politics of personality-cult. The District and Constituency Party activities revolved around the MPs. The branch organisation fell into disuse. At the national level, there was almost fusion between the UPC parliamentary group and the Party's National Council. Following the 1966 crisis, discord permeated

45   *Ideology and Politics in Uganda, 1975,* p143.

through cabinet, Parliament and down to the District Council levels. Normal channels of communication were not readily available. They were diffused. The party leadership appeared to be in great haste to introduce the new ideology and could not wait until the re-organisation of the party structures. The end result was that there was no reliable means of transmitting the aims and objectives of the Move to the Left to the grass roots. And yet these ideological innovations needed to be understood. Most senior cabinet ministers were not well disposed towards the new political culture. The local joke in down town was, 'cabinet ministers carried their hearts on the left and their wallets on the right'. The top and middle cadre officials saw the new ideology as a new threat to the existing political order. There was widespread fear that the new measures would upset the precarious balance of social forces. The well to do, top public civil servants, the landed gentry and not to talk of religious leaders were all seized by the uncertainty of the future. In other words, most possible agents of communication for the new order were not up to it! They were indifferent. To compound matters, the mass media was not sufficiently developed to carry the message on the need for a social revolution. In any case, the majority of Ugandans had, right from the 1950s, been fed on false information about socialism. They were not inclined towards embracing socialism, which was interpreted as communism. One needed to do a lot of spade work to expel fears of socialism that had been planted in the minds of the enlightened few who would in turn have been able to explain to the masses the benefits and merits of nationalisation and the like. That was not possible as the efficiency of the party machinery at grassroots had been impaired.

At the national level, the 1966 crisis left scars on the country's body politic. The changes of 1967 and the new political culture of 1970 opened up old wounds. Prior to the1966 constitutional changes, there existed several power centres at which different groups felt a sense of involvement in the exercise of power. But with the coming into force of the 1967 constitution almost all political power was concentrated at the centre. The former kingdoms and to a certain extent District administrations became mere spectators. They did not have any motivation to propagate among their local population the new government policy as enunciated in the Move to the Left.

The centralisation of power created new problems. The government that was supposed to be the peoples' government became increasingly inaccessible. Decision-making became a preserve of the centre. There was lack of judicious balance of power distribution between the central Government and local authorities. Politically, the new development deprived the centre of constitutional legitimacy. This was more so in Buganda and the kingdoms of the West. The question of concentrating power not only at the centre but also in one person is very much still alive today. Ugandans had hoped that the 1995 constitution would in practice curb the tendency of concentrating power in the hands of one individual. There is evidence to show that the Presidency continues to overshadow and override decisions by parliament. The controversy over the Local Council Act illustrates this point. Equally evident is the fact that parliament has so far vetoed only one appointment proposal submitted by the President for approval. The emergence of a parliamentary caucus composed of the President's "faithful" has greatly eroded the authority of Parliament.

The problem emanates from the general mental attitude of political leaders. There seems to be an inherent urge for 'hero-worship', intensified during the long years of militarism that Ugandans have experienced. The inherent urge for 'hero-worship' is fortified by lack of political conviction, fortitude and proper perception of a civil society. There is also the problem of economic insecurity and greed so that one is exposed to a position of craving for favours from the powers that be. Reduced to such a position one has no alternative but to play the role of a sycophant. Presented with a situation so described, the prospects of genuine democracy in terms of checks and balances in respect of three major arms of government appear to be remote. There is, therefore, great need for men and women who can stand up and be counted on matters of principle. It is also imperative that those entrusted with power must exercise that power judiciously. Men and women in leadership must also understand and appreciate the virtue of tolerance and respect for an opponents point of view. Legitimate dissent must be tolerated.

Apart from political problems outlined above, certain other factors conspired to frustrate the economic measures pronounced at Nakivubo. By the close of 1969, Uganda's economic situation became critical. Because cotton and coffee exports fetched less foreign earnings than in previous years producer prices fell. There was a shortage of imported goods and their prices rose. The Asian traders who dominated the country's commerce, trade, and industry ran amok following the introduction of exchange control in May 1970. Janes H. Mittleman writes:

"Increasingly uncertain about their future in Uganda, Asian businessmen allowed stocks of badly needed supplies to rundown, deposited their funds abroad, engaged in double invoicing and inflation of administrative costs and tempted corrupt officials with bribes… many refused to accept African partners, others paid Africans to act as 'front men' for businesses that remained under the control of their original owners." [46]

Those and other mal-practices frustrated government economic policy. The fall of producer prices and the rocketing prices of essential imported goods had an adverse effect on the ordinary man and woman. They felt the economic squeeze more than anybody else. Opponents of the government, especially those who viewed the Move to the Left with distrust and disfavour, cashed in by spreading disenchantment.

To the extent that the economic standing of the country was critical at the time of launching the ideology innovation, the Move to the Left was ill-timed. This leads me to enquire as to whether A.M. Obote made an educated effort to assess the likely consequences of the proposals contained in the five documents, particularly those pertaining to nationalisation and rationalisation of foreign policy. If he did, what about the mode of presentation and the length of time devoted to propagating the philosophy behind the proposals? I have no doubt that this is an area where things fell apart. As stated earlier, the Party's organisational machinery was in poor shape and totally incapable of propagating the new political culture. The factions at the top had greatly weakened the grass-root organisational structures. At cabinet level many of the ministers had acquired exotic tastes and were quite prepared to defy official policy. Some of the big wigs openly campaigned against the new ideology. In essence the 'Move to the Left' was stillborn. For the innovation ideology to be accepted it was imperative for the Party activists at every level to give it open support and educate the public on its import and implications.

With hindsight it was presumptuous to expect the private sector which was dominated by expatriates whose sympathies lay elsewhere to implement the new economic measures. There was no way such business executives and employees could overnight transfer their loyalty to the government of Uganda.

Turning to the foreign affairs arena, Western powers could not suffer to see Uganda pursue an independent policy that served the country's interests best. When the government of Uganda denied the Israelis access to Northern Uganda to destabilise the government of neighbouring Sudan, Mossad could not stomach it. It may be recalled that strong ties had been established between Uganda and Israel during the 1966/69 period. As

---

46   *Ideology and Politics in Uganda, 1975* pp159-160.

a result of the good diplomatic relationship and the co-operation that existed between the two countries, Israel was able to infiltrate almost all security organs of the Uganda government. Subverting the Army and the Police Force was plain sailing for the agents of the Jewish State. Professor Mahmood Mamdani in his book, *Imperialism and Fascism in Uganda* (1983, pp29-31) quoting the Israel paper 'Ha'aretz', writes:

> "Colonel Bar-Lev, who headed the delegation and is still on good terms with Amin, said that Amin approached him, saying that his loyal supporters were outside Kampala and that the President would be able to arrest and kill him before they could rescue him. Bar-Lev advised Amin to bring to Kampala those soldiers who were from the same tribe as Amin, and to make sure he had paratroopers, tanks and jeeps. So equipped, explained Bar-Lev, 600 men could overpower 5000 men. These forces which had been trained by the Israelis, played a key role in the defeat of Obote's army".

Israel was truly well-placed and the best conduit to promote and to advance the interests of the West.

It remains to point out that Bar-Lev was Chief of the Israeli military team in Uganda in 1971. There were other unprofessional tasks that the Israeli military performed in the aftermath of the coup. Most Ugandan officers who came into contact with the Israelis officials in Uganda in the 1960s will confirm how much the Israeli officials were detested in political circles because of their arrogance, ruthlessness and their complete disregard of other peoples' national pride. Many a time suggestions were made to the Speaker of the National Assembly to send a parliamentary delegation to Israel to see Israel's Knesset at work. As officials of parliament, we tactfully declined the offer without giving any reason. We simply did not approve of Israel agents general behaviour, conduct and the way they went about their 'overt' duties. In 1970 at the United Nations General Assembly I came face to face with an impudent Israeli diplomat who was detailed to solicit African votes on the United Nations resolution condemning Israeli occupation of Arab land. I was a member of the Uganda delegation. The permanent representative had returned to Uganda for consultation. Ambassador Mark Ofwono, accredited to Egypt and myself were standing in for the Head of Mission. Both of us were quite conversant with government policy towards Israel at that material time. So, when we were approached for the Uganda vote, we did not mince words.

We made it clear that Uganda would vote in favour of the UN Security Council Resolution 242 of 1967. Resolution 242 deals with the Arab-Israel conflict and declares that territory is to be given up in return for peace. What did the Israeli mission do? They contacted some junior official in Kampala for clarification. Without knowing the government's stand, their contact assured them that there was no problem. Uganda would vote in favour of Israel. Armed with that information, the official returned to us with instructions to comply with his request. We stuck to our guns. Because of that incident my colleague, the late Mark Ofwono was harassed and molested when he returned to Uganda immediately after the coup of 1971. It would not be far-fetched to conclude that the harassment was instigated by the Israeli officials, who were then chief advisers to Amin. That was the calibre of technical assistance extended to Uganda by the government and people of Israel. While the relationship between Uganda and Israel lasted, Israeli trained personnel and intelligence officers, extended their activities to such fields as agriculture and hotel management. It was a depressing period for a good number of senior government officials who believed in the integrity of Uganda and cherished the sovereignty of their country.

The above account gives in a nutshell an insight into the inherent weaknesses in the formulation of foreign policy and the external forces that conspired to render the implementation of the ideology of modernisation impossible. The military coup staged by Idi Amin Dada on January 25, 1971, deposed Milton Obote as leader of the first UPC elected government. Parliament was dissolved, Political Parties banned and the projected ideological modernisation brought to an abrupt end. The coup d'etat marked the beginning of the gradual economic decline of Uganda and the stagnation of Uganda's social fabric. It also regrettably made the consolidation of militarism possible while the glorification of rule by the gun took a firm root. To date, Ugandans, by and large, remain cowed into submission and find themselves victims of military dictatorship.

Chapter Fourteen

The Rise Of Militarism In Uganda

Post-Independence Africa was characterised by recurrence of military rule. Uganda had its full share in this regard. A brief history of the Uganda army and its impact on the country's political scene will help to understand the tragedy that befell the "Pearl of Africa".

At the time of independence Uganda had within its colonial structure no army to talk about. The military unit known as the Uganda Rifles consisted of a thousand men. Commanding officers of the Rifles were British expatriates. It was, therefore, a pleasant surprise that a Ugandan military officer played the role of an aide-de-camp to the Duke of Kent who represented her Majesty the Queen at the independence celebrations. No doubt, that was a mere public relations exercise. The Ugandan officer in question had just graduated from the prestigious Military Academy, Sandhurst. Faced with the disturbances in the kingdom of Toro by the Bakonjo and Bamba secessionists, cattle rustlers in Karamoja and the unending political turmoil in neighbouring Rwanda, Sudan and the Congo, the military bequeathed to Uganda by the colonialists was too small and ill-equipped for a task of that magnitude.

Accordingly, the government embarked on a programme for the expansion of the army and training of personnel. New equipment was acquired and several barracks established. The programme included sending Ugandans to the United Kingdom for officer cadet course. The number of trained officers increased rapidly. The immediate effect was a growing tension between the Ugandan officers and the expatriates. There was also general anxiety over the method of recruitment into the officer corp. It is important to remember that the composition of the pre-independence military establishment was largely recruited from the northern region with the Acholi taking a lion's share. The ethnic domination of the military throughout the colonial era by the people from the North and up to the time Lt. Col. Museveni shot his way to State House (seat of power) has been one of the most vexed issues that protagonists of the Nilotic-Bantu divide have used as their greatest weapon. But wise counsels remind us that that domination was not a creation of the North. It was a product of partly an accident of history and an unrehearsed colonial policy of unbalanced development. The first major organised contingent of armed men in the history of the "Protectorate" took place in 1893. The new army under Owen MacDonald consisted of over four hundred and twenty Sudanese soldiers and ten thousand Baganda spearmen. The Sudanese soldiers provided the backbone of the new army. It was formed for the campaign against the Kingdom of Bunyoro-Kitara with Kabalega at the helm. The Sudanese soldiers were part of the six hundred mercenaries abandoned in Equatoria in 1889 by Emin Pasha from the Sudan. They were picked up by Captain Lugard somewhere near the south end of Lake Albert, known as Mwitanzige, in 1891. The whole party that included women, children and slaves numbering over eight thousand was moved into Toro where the bulk of the crowd was left to carry out garrison duties against Kabalega's attacks. By 1899 when the Uganda Rifles was formally established under the Uganda Military Forces Ordinance, many of the militia from the South had either moved to eastern Uganda with General Simeon Kakungulu or found their way into the new lucrative hierarchy of chiefs in Buganda.

After the so-called pacification of the country, the colonialists divided the country into zones. They introduced the cultivation of cash crops in the South, which became a plantations zone and declared Acholi, Lango, Teso, West Nile and Kigezi as a reservoir of indentured labour to work in the plantations. In addition, Acholi, Lango and Teso were to serve as a source of military recruitment if and when the need arose to replenish the armed forces.

That explains why by the time of independence most of the men in uniform were drawn largely from Acholi and Lango communities. The practice was reinforced after independence for reasons of political expediency. Attempts were, however, made to create a regional balance at the officer cadre level. Regrettably, the 1966 crisis rendered those efforts useless following a general purge of officers.

The original idea within government framework was to Ugandanise at a gradual pace over a period of a couple of years. That was not to be. The programme was rudely interrupted in January 1964. Suddenly, men of the First Battalion in Jinja staged a mutiny. It was a frustrating and agonising moment. The government of the day made a request to Her Majesty's government for military assistance. British troops were flown in to quell the mutiny. That was the beginning of Uganda's military troubles. The events of January 1964 altered government strategy on defence and security. The mutiny issue was hotly debated in the National Assembly. Members candidly expressed their views on the role of the army visa-a-vis the country's development. Fears were also raised concerning the regional imbalance of the military composition. Nevertheless, the expansion of the Army continued. By 1970 there were four battalions in Jinja, Moroto, Mubende and Mbarara. In addition, there was an Ordinance depot at Magamaga, near Jinja an artillery regiment at Masindi and a reconnaissance regiment was established in Masaka and Mbale. In short, the size of the army grew out of proportion in a period of a few years. All this is made to appear insignificant by the size of Lt. General Museveni's army of the 1990s.

Seven months after the events of January 1964, there was accelerated promotion in the Ugandan army. Shaban Opolot was promoted to the rank of Brigadier. He became commander of the army. Idi Amin was promoted to the rank of Colonel and became Deputy Commander. The author first met the two officers at the Uganda Club, when in his capacity as Secretary to the management committee of the club was asked to process their applications for membership. The Uganda Club was an offshoot of the National Assembly. It was set up in the 1950s principally to cater for members of the Uganda Legislative Council and senior civil servants. The Governor was patron of the club. At one time the club's membership boasted of such personalities as Hereditary Rulers, Paramount Chiefs and outstanding businessmen. The idea was to establish a rendezvous where politicians, top government officials, the elite, the influential and the powerful would meet and exchange views and ideas in a relaxed environment. Hence, there was a need to 'conscript' the newly uplifted heads of the army.

How did the political leadership behave after the mutiny? It is difficult to say. The option was fraternity with the army. Granted the ringleaders of the mutiny were court marshalled, but no steps were taken to examine critically the army as a state institution. The bulk of the army was retained. No benchmarks were put in place to draw a demarcation between civil authority and the military. The relationship between the two remained fluid, bordering on mutual mistrust. Tanzania took a different stand, the entire army was demobilised. An entirely new outfit was established and to counterbalance the army, a national military service was introduced. In Tanzania contours of authority were boldly marked. Civil authority over the military was entrenched. The failure to take a bold stand similar to that of Tanzania cost this country dearly in terms of human life, material resources, economic development and social progress. In the end militarism crept into all sections of Uganda society.

The Minister of Internal Affairs and at the same time in charge of the army, Felix Onama, read the situation correctly when he said, "Our Ugandan officers are therefore plunged into work and responsibility far larger than they expected in the normal course of army career"[47]. However, the available evidence is that the army could have coped with the new military responsibilities with ease and efficiency. What went wrong was that the infant army was reluctantly dragged into the political struggle for state power. The events of 1966 marked the turning point. The arrest and detention of the five cabinet ministers was followed by the arrest of the commander of the army and a general purge of suspected dissident officers and men. From that time the army and the Special Police Force, which was essentially paramilitary, became involved in the work of maintaining law and order which under normal circumstances is the preserve of the Police Force. Since the military coup d'etat of 1971, the military has taken centre stage in the management of public affairs in Uganda.

47   *Uganda Parliamentary Debates (Hansard) Volume 28* p 2060

Chapter Fifteen

Post-Amin Era

"The Pearl of Africa shall rise and shine again" was the slogan of the liberation fighters, who in the 1970s were struggling to oust Idi Amin from power, who had declared himself Life President.

Amin's coup d'etat of 1971 marked a departure from the constitutional and peaceful method of transfer of power through the ballot to that of the barrel of the gun. The military regime instituted by Amin led to the destruction of democratic institutions that the country had worked so hard to put in place. For instance, the legislature, which at the time of the coup had truly become a people's forum for articulating and debating national issues, was abolished. Arbitrary rule replaced the rule of law. The judiciary could no longer perform its function in an atmosphere of impartiality because of intimadation and militarisation of governance. Political parties were castigated and proscribed, party members were harassed, detained or murdered in cold blood with a few escaping into exile. The fate of public officers was no better.

The public service, including the police force and prison services, fell into ruin due to neglect. Amin's intelligence apparatus, the notorious State Research, became the mainstay of Amin's rule of terror. They arrested, detained, tortured and murdered members of the public who were perceived to be enemies of the dictatorship. In the process the moral fabric of society broke down.

Amin's economic policy, the economic war that marked the expulsion of non-Ugandan Asians, depleted the country's foreign reserves, antagonised

Uganda's trade partners, estranged the country from the international financial institutions like the World Bank (WB) and International Monetary Fund (IMF). By the time of the liberation war of 1979 the economy was in total shambles and the infrastructure in complete disrepair.

When the fall of the military dictator became imminent, there arose a general idea in Dar es Salaam that there was need for all groups and organisations of Ugandans opposed to the dictatorship to meet and agree on a strategy for the way forward. That noble idea was developed and led to the Moshi 'Unity' Conference of March 23rd 1979. The Conference lasted for four days. The less said about it the better for the majority of Ugandans who did not experience or hear of the intrigue and underhand activities that took place behind the scenes. Various observations have been made about the Moshi gathering. Some say that it created more problems than it solved while others hold the view that it was a recipe for disaster. Patrick Masette Kuuya, one of the liberation fighters, in his booklet, *A Treatise on Political Stability as a Basis for Another Development for Uganda* (Nyon, Switzerland 1980), describes the Conference thus:

> The original list of groups and individuals invited to the Moshi 'Unity' Conference shows quite clearly that the convenors of the Conference used the word 'unity' in vain. The list contains names of groups and individuals who, except for one minor group (Nairobi), had made no contribution in the war efforts. The minor group was the Uganda Nationalist Organisation (UNO) whose thirty or so men came to Tanzania in November 1978 and by the middle of January 1979, due to adventurous activities and desertions of its fighting wing, had ceased to exist. Three days before the Conference, invitations were sent to some of the groups then fighting. Milton Obote, who was the chairman of nine groups that had come together and were engaged in war efforts, got his invitation two days before the Conference. None of the nine groups had been invited. Yoweri Museveni and Ateker Ejalu who were also leaders of known fighting groups were, like Obote, invited as individuals to bring along with them five delegates. The same right was bestowed on Dan Nabudere and Yash Tandon, who until Moshi, were not leading any group at all.

Eighty Ugandans attended the Conference while over a hundred and fifty were locked out. That is the background to the Conference that resolved to create the Uganda National Liberation Front (UNLF) and the Uganda National Liberation Army (UNLA). The Conference also established the National Consultative Council composed of 30 members. Four Special Committees were appointed, one of which was the Military Commission. An Executive Committee of all members, headed by a chairman, was also put in place. The Chairman was to be ex-official member of the Committee and President of the Third Republic of Uganda.

The task of reconstruction and rehabilitation was not possible under the immediate two Uganda National Liberation regimes of Yusufu Lule and Godfrey Binaisa. Yusufu Lule, imposed on the people by external forces, was a nonentity in the country's body politic, without a political platform or any coherent reconstruction programme. His regime lasted until June 20, 1979 (sixty-eight days). His successor, Godfrey Binaisa did not fare any better except that he ruled for eleven months. Both lacked the capacity to embark on the process of reconstruction and peace-making. Government structures had been destroyed beyond recognition, the economy was in ruins and the leaders did not have the political will to forge ahead with the necessary political and economic reforms. Above all, internal bickering within the ill-assorted National Consultative Council consumed the energy and enthusiasm that had characterised the prosecution of the liberation war.

Yusufu Lule totally failed to appreciate that his accession to the office of the President of the Republic of Uganda was by sheer expediency rather than the process laid down in the 1967 Constitution. His electorate was the NCC and he was expected to abide by the rules of the game drawn up by that body. So, when he insisted that he derived his powers from the Constitution to appoint ministers of his choice, he was deposed on June 20, 1979 by the very organ that nominated him. No amount of demonstration by his tribesmen could save him.

His successor, Godfrey Binaisa, who was 'elected' by 11 votes to 7 met the same fate when he insisted on implementing a resolution passed in April 1980 by the expanded NCC to legalise the UNLF as the only party under which the general elections slated for September were to be held. Both the Democratic Party and the Uganda Peoples Congress vehemently opposed the proposal that came to be known as 'the Binaisa umbrella'.

He was toppled by officers and men of the UNLA in May 1980 and kept under house arrest until the very man he had worked so hard to keep in exile – Apollo M. Obote, released him.

Hours after he was sworn in, the newly elected President detailed this author to get in touch with the detained ex-President and work out with him an appropriate benefits package that was to include housing, monthly allowance, transport, security facilities and the like. I passed on the message to him but got no feedback. The next thing I heard was that he had taken up his post as Vice-Chairman of the Uganda Patriotic Movement. Subsequently, he fled into exile. But in 1985, shortly after the coup by General Tito Okello, I met him briefly in Nairobi. He was homebound and told me that he had been beckoned by the General to return to Uganda and that he wanted to be rehabilitated. All he got was a soldier as an escort. Because he moved on foot with his uniformed escort, the impression created downtown was that he was a prisoner!

Opportunity must be taken at this juncture to pay tribute to Mwalimu Julius Nyerere, the then President of Tanzania not only for committing Tanzanian troops during the liberation war but for the crucial role he played at the most critical moment when Uganda was on the verge of collapse. I shall always remember him as an honest broker. It was through his efforts, together with the Military commission composed of a rare brand of nationalists and dedicated Ugandans, that Uganda was able to stand on her own and restore a semblance of law and order, leading to the 1980 elections. Members of the Military Commission were:

Mr Paulo Muwanga (Chairman)
Mr Yoweri Museveni (Vice-Chairman)
Major General Tito Okello (Commander of Defence Forces)
Brigadier David Oyite Ojok (Chief of Staff)
Colonel William Omaria (Deputy Minister of Defence)
Colonel Zed Maruru (Staff: Ministry of Defence)

In the 1980 elections held under the multi-party system, the major political parties that participated were the Conservative Party (CP), the Democratic Party (DP), the Uganda Peoples Congress (UPC) and the Uganda Patriotic Movement (UPM). The parties were led by Joshua Mayanja Nkangi, Paulo K. Ssemogerere, Apollo Milton Obote and Yoweri K. Museveni, respectively. There were 126 parliamentary seats to be contested. The DP and UPC contested all the seats. The CP and the UPM could not cover all the constituences. The UPM under the leadership of Yoweri Museveni only managed to raise 76 candidates. The DP was not able to produce polling agents to cover 5000 or so polling stations. The election results were as follows: UPC 74, DP 51, UPM 1 and CP nil. It is worth noting that DP swept the board in Buganda although no

UPC candidate lost any deposit (the money one has to pay before filing nomination papers), signifying a substantial following in the region.

Immediately after the declaration of the results, leaders of the Democratic Party and the Uganda Patriotic Movement began peddling lies that the elections had been rigged. Fears of possible rigging had been raised earlier on in the regular meeting of leaders and representatives of all political parties organised by the Military Commission to enable intending participant political parties to work out electoral procedures and and to iron out contentious issues. In order to allay those fears, the Chairman of the Military Commission agreed to invite a Commonwealth Observers Group to oversee the elections and to submit a report. Terms of reference of the Observer Group were spelt out as follows:

- The Observer Group will observe every relevant aspect of the organisation and conduct of the elections by the Electoral Commission in accordance with the laws of Uganda relating to elections.
- Their function will be to ascertain in their impartial judgement whether, in the context of the law, the elections have been free and fair.
- On furtherance of this objective, it will be competent for the group to bring to the attention of the Electoral Commission or the Uganda authorities from time to time such matters as they consider pertinent.

The Group was constituted in London (Headquarters of the Commonwealth of Nations) on November 21 and arrived in Kampala four days later. Members of the Commonwealth Observer Group were drawn from Australia, Barbados, Botswana, the United Kingdom, Canada, Cyprus, India and Siera Leone. The Chairman of the Group was Ambassador Kojo Debrah of Ghana.

According to the Group, the electoral process, despite a rugged economy, a precarious law and order situation and a shattered communication system, was quite satisfactory. In the circumstances, the 1980 elections were declared free and fair. Despite the clearance by the Commonwealth Observers Group, disgruntled elements refused to accept defeat. One such person was Yoweri Museveni who could not contain the frustration and the only elected member of UPM did not even take his seat in Parliament. That Y. K. Museveni opted for violence in the face of electoral defeat did not come as a surprise for those who cared to monitor the country's political trend and events following the Moshi Conference. The New

Vision of November 26, 1990 reported President Museveni as having told a gathering that he began to plot for taking over the government of Uganda by force in 1979 and that he recruited some men for the purpose. During the time he was Minister of Defence under Yusufu Lule and Godfrey Binaisa he abused his office by recruiting his kinsmen into UNLA and who eventually formed the core of his National Resistance Army in the bush. His reaction after the defeat was predictable because he had declared as early as July 1979, "...I think the majority of the Ugandan people want a new political force which does not feature the elements of those who are responsible for the past mistakes. I do not think that having to choose between Obote and Amin is a pleasant choice for many Ugandans. What many people want is a fresh beginning..." (Taken from his interview reported by Forward magazine – No. 3 of July 1979.)

The people of Uganda did not have to choose between Obote and Amin in the 1980 elections. They were presented with a much wider choice. In the first instance the choice was not based on individual merit. The choice was based on different political platforms, with alternative political programmes. The electorate rejected the Uganda Patriotic Movement, which Museveni headed mainly because UPM produced no manifesto and was too feeble on the ground to be entrusted with the enormous task of rehabilitation that lay ahead. The majority of Ugandans preferred the Uganda Peoples Congress because they were familiar with the party's capacity and commitment to serve them. Museveni's alternative was the path of violence, which up till now, he continues to traverse.

The bush war was launched on February 6, 1981. Museveni is also known not to have been keen on holding elections in 1980. His argument was that the Military Commission regime needed consolidation. He was, however, overruled by his colleagues who insisted that the Military Commission was an interim arrangement to get the country back to a popular government. Not only did Museveni reject the election results but he also abandoned the only constitutional option for any law-abiding citizen found in such a situation i.e. proceeding to the courts of law for redress. Since he personally lost the election he could have submitted a petition to the High Court to that effect. But to do so one needed concrete evidence, which was not available. The fact is that votes were counted at the polling stations immediately after the closure of the polls and every candidate was expected to have a polling agent to ensure that he countersigned the necessary papers after the count. Instead, Museveni opted for launching a bush war against the people of Uganda and the newly elected government. It is my contention that if terrorism is defined by the nature of the act and, not by the identity of the perpetrators or the nature of their cause, then Museveni's bushwar was a terrorist act and the perpetrators of that war were terrorists despite their pretentious claims. That their motives were political and were an organised group proved a true hallmark of terrorism. That war plunged the country back into mayhem of bloodshed, devastation and senseless destruction never experienced before. The country witnessed an influx of armed dissidents. It began with Alice Lakwena's Holy Spirit Army (HSA) in the North followed by Uganda People's Army (UPA) of Peter Otai in the East, the Uganda Rescue Front 11 (UNRF) under Ali Bamwoze in West Nile, the Allied Defence Forces (ADF) in Western Region and then Itongwa's Uganda Freedom Army in Buganda. The war by the Lord's Resistance Army of Joseph Kony that started in 1987 was the most vicious and enduring. It was only after great pressure was brought to bear on both sides that they agreed to talk peace. Although the talks were inconclusive, there is today relative peace in Northern Uganda.

What is of interest is why Museveni chose to launch the war in Luwero District and not in the constituency where the DP candidate defeated him. There are many reasons. He had to choose an area that was totally under the control of the opposition. Luwero District was in Buganda, a DP dominated region and with Yusufu Lule's disgruntled elements drawn from the old Mengo establishment. The second reason was that Luwero District had a large population of people from Rwanda of Tutsi origin who came to Uganda as immigrant workers or refugees. Rwandese residents were then settled as herdsmen, farm labourers and house servants. Most of these abandoned their employers and joined the National Resistance Army (NRA). It was that group of ex-employees who served as guides (called *abalebesi* in Luganda) to various homesteads in search of food and other supplies without any payment. To be able to do all that with ease, Museveni had to rid the District of the northern resident ethnic group. The bandits targeted their homes and food granaries and forced them to flee. It was indeed this group that alerted people in the neighbouring districts about what was happening in Luwero and as a result bandits were not welcome in other parts of Buganda. Hence, the bandits were confined to the Luwero Triangle.

The claim that the bush war was launched with only 27 men is preposterous. Such a small number of men could not have covered the entire District in such a short period of time and rained so much havoc.

After creating panic and subduing the population at large the rebels embarked on intensive and aggressive recruitment by killing the old and the weak and forcing the young men into the ranks of bandits. An advance unit of rebels disguised as government troops would attack a given village, cause havoc as if they were looking for insurgents. Then another unit of bandits would arrive, offer sympathy and condolences to the survivors and persuade them to evacuate the area and move to the zones under their control. This is what befell this author's relatives who were abducted somewhere along the Kampala /Hoima road. The two adults together with their children spent three years in captivity until they were rescued by government troops and placed in the resettlement camps at Katera trading centre 50 miles from Kampala.

Atrocities were committed against innocent citizens. Nobody would imagine that the NRA rebels in the execution of the bush war were using 'rubber bullets'. As stated above, there is evidence to show that hundreds of innocent people were forcibly driven from their homes in the villages and held as hostages. Many of the hostages perished in the process. There was also the urban brigade whose members committed the most heinous crimes against the citizenry. They robbed banks, stole motor vehicles, broke into government hospitals and grabbed anything they came across. In short, they terrorised the urban population and killed people indiscriminately.

As already pointed out, the NRA technique of recruitment entailed invading and attacking a given village under the disguise of government troops to create panic and fear among villagers. That is one of the attributes of terrorism. The old and the weak would be killed. Later on the same bandits would return and force the residents to areas under the control of the rebels. The youth would be conscripted into the rebel ranks. Most of the youth so conscripted were orphans whose parents would have been deliberately eliminated. Because these children were young and small, they came to be known as *kadogos*. Kadogo is a Swahili word for small; in other words, child soldiers.

It was easy to win the support of these youngsters because they were told that their parents had been killed by government troops. To them, fighting against government was some sort of revenge against the killers of their parents. They became a formidable force because youths have a strong propensity for instant gratification – wanting all and wanting it fast.

The wanton use of child soldiers did not end with NRM assumption of power. On the contrary, it was the *kadogo* soldiers who were the first victims of the war in the Nothern Region of the country. It is estimated that about four thousand of them perished in that senseless war that raged on for nearly twenty years. As a matter of fact, children have been dragged into all major conflicts that have taken place in the Great Lakes region, particularly in the Democratic Republic of Congo and in Southern Sudan.

There is no doubt that one of the key features of the NRM bush war was the pioneering of the massive use of child soldiers in the Graet Lakes Region. Since the future, to a large extent, belongs to the youth, it is imperative that the youth should be fully integrated into the social, economic and political life of their country of origin. That objective cannot be achieved if children continue to be used to fight wars. Children need a stable, harmonious and quiet environment at all ages. Above all, children need affection and care, that universal sentiment, to be able to develop a balanced personality. A child soldier misses family, does not go to school and is therefore unable to interact in a conducive environment so essential in the development of one's personality.

One of the agonies inflicted in the Great Lakes Region by the senseless wars is the emergence of street children with the attendant social evils of drugs, prostitution and armed robbery. It is hoped that future African governments will endeavour, through the auspices of the African Union, to implement the provisions of the Convention on the Rights of the Child as adopted by the General assembly of the United Nations on November 20, 1989.

It is difficult to believe that such acts of murder; destruction of property and armed robbery could have been carried out by a group of rational and civilised men. As if that was not enough, NRM staged a *coup de grace* by putting on show skulls of the departed souls - men and women who were victims of the bush war. There is something strange about the public exhibition of human skulls- the practice is a non-indigenous Ugandan custom. Indeed, that must have been a group of men and women with 'extraordinary and uncouth impulse of passion'. Anybody with a conscience is aghast at the crude methods employed in the execution of that bush war.

Details of the rebel activities began to be revealed in 1982 by young men and women who had been rescued by UNLA after storming the headquarters of the Uganda Freedom Movement (UFM) under Andrew Kayira who had earlier on tried in vain to storm Lubiri Barracks. Yusufu Lule was the overall Chairman of the organisation. The rescued persons came to be known as "human computers" because of the amount of information they were able to give to the army. That is how government learnt about heneous acts of the terror perpetrated by the bandits.

Reports from sources of Obote II officials indicate that when government troops captured areas previously occupied by NRA, thousands and thousands of people were found at the point of death. Mothers, together with their young children, were rushed to reception centres and then to hospitals. The Italian government funded the rehabilation of a clinic at Mulago set aside to cater for the sick mothers and their children. My relatives spent a week at the clinic.

The government appointed a retired ex-British expatriate to coordinate relief assistance of Non-Government Organisations interested in rehabilitation of displaced persons living in temporary camps. It was at that juncture that Museveni fled to Sweden. That, in brief, is the other side of the Luwero Triangle story.

We need a Truth and Reconciliation Commission to establish exactly what took place.

When NRA took power in January 1986, a number of organs were established. The National Resistance Council (NRC) was one of such organs. The elections of 1989 for the expansion of NRC were in actual fact internal elections to an NRM organ and not a general election. The mode adopted in those elections was not through universal adult suffrage and not by secret ballot. It was through electoral colleges that made the electorate extremely restricted. The type of candidature at these indirect elections marked the introduction of the "personal merit' concept that was to become the regime's centre pin in the entrenchment of its rule.

The interim period of NRM regime was unilaterally extended for five years. At the same time the initial broad base of the regime was narrowed by dropping several members of the regime's partners, namely, the DP.

The NRM was then in a position to unfold and embark on the implementation of its hidden agenda. The first stage of the programme was the appointment of a Constitutional Commission without consulting other political forces in the country. The effect was that the non-movement political forces were not represented on the Commission.

The deliberate omission of non-movement political forces on the commission made it easy for NRM to impose their own pre-conceived ideas on the type of constitution they wanted to draw up. The situation was compounded by the fact that the activities of political parties were banned, in particular, by denying them the right to convene public meetings. That way the parties were effectively incapacitated and did not, therefore, mobilise their members and the public at large did not debate the terms of reference of the constitutinal commission or collect evidence from their members and the public for submission to the commission.

On the other hand, the regime was free to disseminate their views on the movement system through Resistance Council (RC) meetings, public rallies, seminars and workshops. In effect the memoranda and resolutions submitted to the constitutional commission that claimed to be views of the people of Uganda were the product of the RC meetings, public rallies, seminars and workshops organised by the regime.

In this type of political environment, the findings and the recommendations of the commission were predictable. The country is now saddled with a constitution, which embraces the political philosophy of the movement practised during the ten years of the so-called interim period. The system is nothing more than a mechanism to preserve and entrench dictatorship by ensuring that organised competitive politics is eliminated from Uganda's body politic.

The new constitution legitimized a one-party state under which Fundamental Human Rights and Freedom of Association of Assembly were proscribed under articles 269 and 270. Under the said articles and the Political Organisation Act 2002, political parties were divorced from the grass roots and are not allowed to contest elections to public institutions and offices. They were not in a position to convene and address public meetings on any matter of public interest. In short, parties were placed in cold storage. Luckily, the obnoxious articles have since been repealed under the dispensation of multiparty system.

This is testimony to the objective of NRM/A revolution as spelt out in paragraph 3.3 of their document entitled: "THE NRM / A REVOLUTION" which states that other political parties, namely UPC, DP, CP and NLP will cease to exist as required by the revolution. It is now clear that the Movement, the Referendum and the Political Organisation Acts are part of the secret agenda and, in effect, a *coup de grace* of the implementation of "NRM / A REVOLUTION".

Since Museveni's accession to power the country has been deprived of any enjoyment of meaningful peace in the normal sense of the word. There is no peace of mind among the population. Besides, war raged on in the northern, eastern and western regions of the country for a very long time. An entirely new culture of guerrilla warfare engulfed Uganda. The country is plagued by a host of social evils: corruption, robbery, defilement, drug addiction, etc. The people of Luwero, his centre of operation, were devastated, their property destroyed and survivors of the war reduced to living under the most inhuman conditions. In another development, in an effort to pacify the North and the East, thousands of innocent people lost their lives. There was extensive deliberate destruction of property under the "scorch earth" operation and complete disregard for life reminiscent of the colonial wars perpetrated against Ugandans in the last century. The net result was loss of so many lives, so much deprivation, devastation and squander of such great resources on prosecution of internal wars never seen before in the history of Uganda. The majority of the inhabitants of the Districts of Gulu, Kitgum and Pader continued to live in makeshift camps (the notorious Protected Villages). Even within the camps security was not guaranteed. It was misery everywhere. The greatest surprise being that the world at large looked on unconcerned.

The bush war was ostensibly launched and waged under the banner of returning the country to a system of democratic governance. Today the country is over-burdened with a dictatorship of a clique that is determined to impose its will on the population. The clique under the name of the national movement manipulated the 1995 constitution extensively and went ahead to rig the subsequent presidential and parliamentary elections of 1996 and 2001, 2006 through intimidation and bribery.

Slovo, the South African freedom fighter and an avowed communist aptly predicts the consequences of a monolithic system of governance when he asserts, "The single party state except at rare moments in history is a recipe for tyranny. What we have learnt from the Soviet experience and the African experience is that the concept of the party as a vanguard which has a right by virtue of calling itself something and which is entrenched in the constitution as a permanent godfather of this society, is a disaster" (Slovo 1995, pp14-15). It follows that the much needed unity, political stability, economic development and social progress in this country remain elusive and untenable until the basic freedoms and rights of association, assembly and expression and, above all, opportunity to vote for a government of one's choice in a free and fair election are encouraged and allowed to grow and flourish.

Members of the Constituent Assembly when discussing the 1995 Constitution felt unable to define 'National Resistance Movement' in concrete terms. Nevertheless, political scientists and opinion leaders in Uganda, who have followed the activities of the movement and its method of work for seemingly endless years, are agreed that the movement answers to the description of a faction defined by James Madison, one of the authors of the Federalist Papers (The Federalist Papers, The New York Times Co. 1962) who later became the fourth president of the United States of America uses the term 'faction' to describe 'an ambitious group (religious, political or economic) actuated by some common impulse of passion of interest, adverse to the rights of some citizens, or to the permanent and aggregate interests of the community". The National Resistance Movement regime that was born out of violence, as indicated above, fits that description.

The movement seeks to impose an artificial uniformity on a plural society. Political parties and other political forces are required to conform to a single view, 'the correct line' to use the movement jargon. In order to impose its will on all other political organisations, the movement has to rely heavily on the state coercive apparatus as was the case in the colonial time after the 1945-49 riots and the post-independence period in the aftermath of the 1966 crisis. That, of course, will mean repression that may result in armed conflict. The silent majority insist that Uganda needs a government that permits a variety of viewpoints, a government that shuns extremism and a government totally committed to the exercise of power with restraint. They argue that the notion of 'power by elites' is an affront to democratic institutions because the isolated rational individual must be related to other social groups, political parties and the totality of the social environment. The idea of basing politics on individual merit is erroneous and counter-productive and it must be rejected if peace and stability are to prevail.

The individual merit arrangement designed by the NRM does not allow any room or provide a political platform for public discussion of issues of critical national importance. It does not offer an opportunity for a critical assessment and evaluation of competence and credibility of aspiring candidates outside the organs and ambit of NRM. Election campaign based on individual merit is devoid of matters of national policy leading to alternative development plans or strategy at the national level. Individual merit politics deprive the country of organised opposition interest groups, especially political parties that would otherwise play the role of watchdog over the day to day activities and performance of the government.

In practical terms, the ultimate effect of "Individual merit" does not affect in any way or threaten the positions of the movement leadership at the top of the hierarchy. In other words, no change can be brought about through individual merit. That explains why Colonel Kizza Besigye's sudden challenge in the 2001 Presidential elections created such panic and wreaked havoc within the Movement circles. In sum, personal merit is designed to protect and preserve personal rule in public affairs and negates all known attributes of democratic governance.

Personal merit has not only compounded Uganda's perennial problem of decision-making at the highest level of government but has also hampered a possible evolution of viable decision making process. Authorities in Uganda have for a long time lacked adequate decision-making mechanisms. The absence of such mechanisms may be attributed to a number of factors such as Milton Obote's high degree of inability throughout his stewardship to deal expeditiously with sensitive and often explosive political issues. His reluctance to take swift and firm action against the characters engaged in various conspiracies leading to the 1966 crisis illustrates the point at issue. He also totally failed to deal with the plotters of the 1971 military coup. History repeated itself in the early 1980s when Yoweri Museveni and his clique launched an armed rebellion against the people of Uganda in order to impose personal rule. It has taken the population a period of many years of suffering to discover that the clique simply took the country for a ride.

The Lutwa debacle of 1985 was a result of a similar pattern of procrastination. It took the appointing authority, that is, the president over one year to fill the post of Chief of Staff, following the tragic death of Major General Oyite Ojok in a helicopter crash in the Luwero triangle bush war. The delay in filling the vacant post gave ample time to the consipirators to plan and organise themselves.

Worse still, the man at the helm abandoned established government institutions in search of a resolution and resorted to the Langi and Acholi college of elders. The outcome was a disaster not only for the two communities but for the entire population of Uganda who had absolutely nothing to do with the quarrels and rivalry of the two communities. In the process, he lost the ability to determine the consequences of the conflict. He ought to have considered seriously Henry Kissinger's advice that the public does not forgive its leaders for disasters.

The unprecedented habit of Uganda's heads of state to spend most of their time dealing with secondary issues that are administrative in nature has fostered and cultivated the culture of personality-cult. In the process ministers have since the Amin regime abdicated their responsibilities of taking decisions on matters that fall squarely under the jurisdiction of their portfolios. The tendency is to shift responsibility to the "BIG MAN" under the guise of seeking clearance. In fact, under the presidential cum parliamentary system that obtains in Uganda, one would only be obliged to seek clearance from the office of the President on major issues and then obtain approval of the cabinet.

That has not always been the case. The overall effect of the ministers' inability or reluctance to take prompt action on matters of policy and the tendency to refer minor or purely matters arising from settled policies to the Head of State has not only contributed to the culture of personality-cult but has encouraged the false idea of indispensability of the reigning Head of State. The regimes of 'Life President' Amin and Lt. General Museveni have given credence to this practice to the point of absurdity.

A major defect in the decision-making process has been a glaring lack of an effective monitoring system. In theory the cabinet secretariat could have played the role of monitoring the implementation of major cabinet decisions. But the cabinet secretariat is too small, under- staffed and ill-equipped for the purpose. Besides, it has no legal framework under which to exercise that authority. The ranking of the secretariat in terms of structural hierarchy remains too low to guarantee compliance. Accountability and transparency in terms of furnishing written returns or reports by line ministries is not something that cabinet ministers are inclined to encourage. Time and again the author while serving as Secretary to the Cabinet experienced great difficulty in obtaining returns from ministers promptly. Unfortunately, he received no encouragement to improve the monitoring system.

On the other side of the pendulum lies the high-handedness of Idi Amin and Yoweri Museveni exhibited in making major decisions without consultation. In the circumstances implementers are hard put to explain such decisions to the public. The effect of non-involvement of implementers in the process of decision-making begets incoherence, lack of consistency and ultimately the "I don't care attitude". Needless to say, decisions taken without due consultation cannot reflect well thought out policy choices. Lt. General Y. K. Museveni's State House staff (read kitchen cabinet) has no capacity to study and analyse issues of national importance.

Under his style of leadership, his approach to national issues does not permit public debate on both sides of the argument. Official political opposition is disregarded.

The most perturbing aspect of the Lt. General's style of administration is that he does not believe in the concept of limitation of powers. In other words, he recognises no limits to power. That is why on two occasions he ordered the Uganda People's Defence Forces to go beyond our borders into neighbouring territories. He is Uganda's Louis XIV "L etat, c'est moi" (I am the state).

Consequently, the denial of any limit of powers has led to disaster after disaster e.g. the huge cost of human life in the Democratic Republic of Congo, and the destruction of human life and property in Northern Uganda. The result is that by the beginning of the new millennium, he stood alone and exhausted. He refuses to accept that change is the law of life. He has totally failed to transform his political will and dominance into a sense of shared obligations thereby casting a cloud of gloom and uncertainty over the future of our country.

Chapter Sixteen

The Future

"You learn the past to define the future." – (Confucius).

Posterity will definitely want to know why Uganda's elaborate experiment in democratic governance failed. The reasons are many and they differ from one group to another depending on the political philosophy and orientation of the concerned group or individual. The following account attempts to give an impartial point of view as to why the democratisation process modelled on the British Westminster type of government failed. The concept of democracy in these lines includes the system of constitutional and democratic governance universally accepted. We have seen when dealing with Uganda's history of political development that lack of a central political forum impeded progress towards national political consciousness and the establishment of unity by the indigenous people of Uganda. The Legislative Council popularly known as LEGCO was established on June 29, 1920 and for the next twenty five long years remained an exclusive club of white expatriates who were joined in the late 1920s by the Asian immigrants. The Africans eventually found access to the Council in 1945. The three African nominees were drawn from Buganda, the western and eastern provinces. From Buganda came the Katikiro (Prime Minister) nominated by the Kabaka. The western province nominee was in rotation, the Katikiro of the kingdoms of Bunyoro, Toro and Ankole. The third nominee represented the Eastern Province again in rotation the Secretary- General of the districts of Busoga, Bugisu, Bukedi and Teso. Three years later a fourth African member joined his colleagues to represent the Northern Province. It is important to note that the four African members of the council were high ranking chiefs. Their presence in the Council did nothing to mitigate the overall political condition of the ordinary African. In other words, they were not representatives of the people. Their membership was a mere extension of chieftainship to the Council. They were there to ensure that British interests were secured in view of the political upheavals that were taking place in other parts of the empire, notably, in Asia and West Africa.

Ten years later some nationalists crept into the Council when its membership was increased to sixty, fifty percent of whom were Africans. The fifty percent consisted of African representatives nominated by the various District councils. Buganda sent five representatives. The rest of the African members were nominated by the Governor and took their seats on government benches. The Buganda representatives were a novelty in the history of the Council. The five representatives happened to be members of the Uganda National Congress- that mother of political parties. They were nominated by the Lukiko acting as an electoral college. That was in the aftermath of the return of the Kabaka from exile. The Namirembe Agreement of 1955 required Buganda to make a firm undertaking that it would participate in the Legislative Council. The undertaking notwithstanding, Buganda pulled out of the Council in 1958 on technicalities following the appointment of a Speaker to preside over the Council's deliberations in place of the Governor. Buganda contended that the appointment of the Speaker was in breach of the Namirembe Agreement, which stipulated that no major political changes were to take place before 1961.

Buganda's withdrawal from LEGCO was a great blow to the steady progress towards building a national forum for the people Uganda. Despite these draw-backs, the people from the rest of the country were determined to cast away foreign rule and achieve independence. So, African representatives in concert with non-African representatives pressed ahead. They formed a Representatives Members Organisation - a precursor of a Parliamentary Opposition. The handful of African members had by 1960 gained a great deal of experience in parliamentary procedures. They acquired some insight into the running of a modern government machinery. Above all, they helped raise the level of national consciousness from the previous narrow vision based on "nationalities". The limited 1958 direct elections to LEGCO widened that vision. The brief history of the Legislative Council does emphasise the fact that Ugandan politicians had no means of interaction in an institutionalised manner until the mid-1950s. The formation of national political parties came too late and when established there was lack of trained managerial manpower. The parties had no resources to maintain proper organisation. The few educated elite were, more often than not, absorbed in the local government administrations and the Central Government Civil Service.

The infant political organisations could not count on the business community for financial support. The economy was under the control of aliens whose interests were in sharp contradiction with the political aspirations of the Africans. In areas where a few Africans managed to penetrate trade and commerce, that is, in southern Uganda and the midland, political parties were not enthusiastically welcome. Because there was no single political organ strong enough and no adequate funds for mobilisation, it was difficult to sensitise the population and arouse national consciousness. Political activities did not go beyond the boundaries of individual nationalities. Buganda, which was the largest administrative unit, took advantage of the absence of a viable national forum to advance and entrench the interests of the landed gentry. In the process the Western Region kingdoms and to a lesser extent other districts did their best to emulate Buganda. Indeed, by the time of the pre-independence conference held in London Buganda played the role of a standard bearer. Hence, the need for the ill-assorted assembly of delegates drawn from all corners and sections of the country. While in British India negotiations for independence were carried out by the Indian Congress Party and The Muslim League, Uganda's major political parties, the UPC and DP were not able to stand in for the whole of Uganda. No special status was accorded to them, except that the UPC was in government and the DP was the official Opposition. Their mandate was limited. No undisputed political leader had yet emerged. The keynote was "nationality" and not nation. In line with what has been outlined above, James H. Mittleman appears to sum up aptly Uganda's political ills when he says: "Given the traditional rivalries, the fragmentation and the inflexibilities of politics in Uganda… it is certain that following independence, Uganda, like any other country, suffered from lack of power in both relative and absolute terms". [48] The lack of unity of purpose is another problem that nagged and haunted political leaders. The snag emanated from the system of indirect rule introduced by the British in the agreement areas of Ankole, Buganda, Bunyoro and

48   *Ideology and Politics in Uganda* 1975 (P83).

Toro that kept political activities at the periphery of these kingdoms. The king's subjects looked at the Governor (although vested with executive powers) as a high priest who was there to receive petitions and resolve complaints submitted to him. Within the kingdoms the hereditary rulers were the fountain of justice and dispensers of benefits. In discharging these "responsibilities" the hereditary rulers were assisted by top traditional chiefs, the Katikiro/Enganzi (Prime Minster); the Omulamuzi (Chief Judge), and the Omuketo/Muwanika (Treasurer). The kingdoms had their own mini parliaments, the Rukurato in Bunyoro and Toro, the Lukiko in Buganda and the Ishengyero in Ankole. There were District Commissioners to supervise the work of chiefs on behalf of the Central Government. The District Commissioners in the kingdoms, except in Buganda, continued to wield tremendous powers as representatives of the Central Government. In the non-kingdom areas of the North and the East, the British established direct rule. However, in places where paramount chiefs existed they played the role of intermediaries between the District Commissioners and the local people. In the final analysis the District Commissioners took a more active role in the day to day administration of the districts.

Indirect Rule

The principle of indirect rule became a subject of a lively debate within the colonial administration circles at the beginning of the Second World War. The majority of the colonial administrators were still committed to the chiefs and were suspicious of the worth and representative nature of the urban nationalists. They believed that election of representatives would shift the balance of power within the African community in favour of the nationalists. On the other hand, men like Sir Bernard Bourdillion, Governor of Nigeria, argued; "if an alien bureaucracy can govern through the agency of indigenous institutions, there appears to be no valid reasons why native central government should not do the same".[49] But down the line he missed the point and forgot to insist that "agency" should be democratised. Lord Hailey had a better perception. He says: "The principle of indirect rule, if not compatible with the ideal of self government, representative institutions are at all events so alien to it that native institutions must be materially modified if they are to fit in any scheme involving an electoral Parliament".[50]

---

49   Sir Bernard Bourdillon Governor of Nigeria- *Memorandum On The Future Political Development Of Nigeria, Lagos* 1939 (P5).
50   *The African Survey, London* 1938 (P 1640).

The colonial policy advocated by Sir Bernard Bourdillon and Lord Hailey were the antithesis of the proclamation made by the governor of Uganda in 1941. Sir Charles Dundas reinforced the doctrine of indirect rule when he declared in his memorandum On Native Administration in Uganda that he desired to make the position on duties of the Resident more in accord with the intention of the Agreement than had been in the past. The Agreement stipulated that 'the Kabaka should exercise direct rule subject to the King's overrule' which was of course delegated to the Governor. For that reason the Resident could not have the authority nor fulfil the functions of a Provincial Commissioner. His duty was not to direct affairs or to control the Kabaka's officials but to advise the Kabaka's government and the Governor in the exercise of his authority. But since he could not direct and control he could not assume responsibility for the actions of the Kabaka's government and its servants. That responsibility lay with His Highness the Kabaka acting on the advice of his council of ministers subject to the Governor's overriding powers. The Governor explained further that in the past, it was necessary for the British administration to go beyond those limits and take part in detailed inspections of the work of the Kabaka's chiefs. That meant, however, that the chiefs were under two masters and the people, particularly in the more distant parts of Buganda, looked to the District Commissioners as much to the Kabaka's government for adjustment of their affairs.

Recognising that there had been a dual administration in Buganda which was perhaps necessary, the Governor declared that the stage had been reached for the Protectorate Government not to go beyond the scope set by the Agreement in the way of supervision of the Kabaka's Administration . He was emphatic that he did not wish to perpetuate a system that was not contemplated when the Agreement was concluded. He, therefore, directed that the Resident and his staff were to confine themselves to advice and guidance, leaving inspection and control to the Kabaka's government and its agents.

That was it. The governor's directive was retrogressive in terms of building national institutions. The significance of the governor's directive to the Mengo establishment was the granting of autonomy to Buganda. The autocratic Mengo establishment from then onwards was not prepared to surrender that political autonomy to anybody or any organisation of a national character. It was that spirit of separatism that sparked off Buganda's refusal to participate in the Legislative Council and the eventual boycott of the 1961 elections. Professor Kenneth Ingham in his book sums up Buganda's situation thus: "At midnight on December 31, 1960, Buganda declared its independence. The British administration dismissed the announcement as preposterous and within a few days the announcement was forgotten, but the gesture was profoundly significant. The Ganda leaders had not been primarily concerned with ridding their country of imperial rule. There was already every indication that the British were planning to quit Uganda in the future without prompting from within. What Buganda wished to do was to pre-empt that moment by establishing its independence before the rest of the Protectorate. A situation which was initially tolerable over British overrule had, in the eyes of Buganda's leaders, become rapidly less so since the Second World War. In their estimation it would become wholly intolerable <u>if the kingdom were to become a minority element in a united independent Uganda - outvoted in parliament over questions of sovereignty</u> -(the emphasis is mine), with its economic pre-eminence challenged by envious rivals". [51] Forty years earlier, Sir Apollo Kaggwa had expressed similar sentiments which were echoed by the Katikiro of Buganda Michael Kintu in 1960 to the effect that from time immemorial, the Baganda had known no other rule above their Kabaka in his kingdom, and still they did not recognise anybody whose authority did not derive from the Kabaka and was exercised on his behalf.

Similar arguments were advanced from time to time whenever the colonial central government took measures towards developing Uganda as one country. That was the argument that continued to be advanced up to the time of independence when Buganda flatly refused direct election of her representatives to the National Assembly. Such statements emphatically sealed the operations and activities of political parties in Buganda. There were obvious political implications. It was that type of thinking that held up for a long time the integration of Buganda into the political life of the whole country. The situation was compounded by the failure of the colonial administration to allow African participation in the Central Government in the early stages of political development. Worse still, the colonial administration harboured great contempt for nationalists when they finally emerged in the mid-1940s. The nationalists were regarded as rogues, men without any political acumen or administrative skills who had no influence on the population, especially in the rural areas. The constitutional reforms of 1955 came a bit too late. In the words of Low

51   *Politics in Modern Africa: The uneven tribal dimension* 1990 Routledge, London (Chapter 2, P12).

and Pratt: "The constitutional reforms of 1955 left the final development of Uganda's political development an open question-only the efforts of Uganda nationalists against the dividing strands of their inherited traditions can finally assure a united democratic Uganda".

Factional disputes in Acholi, Bukedi, Bugisu and Toro re-emerged immediately after independence. Another source of friction has been tension between different religious groups often manifested in political alignment. For a long time, political parties exhibited a religious divide. Catholics were presumed to belong to the Democratic Party while Protestants, now members of the Church of Uganda were dubbed Uganda Peoples Congress supporters. Down the line Moslems were condemned to the periphery to serve once in a while the interests of the main stream religious groups. Many a politician exploited this weakness to the point of absurdity, especially among the illiterate masses. Ugandan political leaders are yet to learn that government depends on consent, compromise and a willingness to see others' point of view in matters large and small. It was the hope of all Ugandans that political leaders would after independence nurture and foster rationalisation that would breed a wider loyalty to the nation as opposed to local loyalties and personal interests.

In addition to the dividing strands of the traditions inherited by the nationalists, new factors have come into play, militarism being the most significant.

The army was sharply divided along ethnic lines between the Bantu of the South and the Nilotics of the North. Whether the divide was imaginary or real, it brought about a real political polarisation particularly in Kampala and the surrounding areas. The military attack on the Kabaka's palace at Mengo was the last straw. That the army was used to settle an essentially political matter created a dangerous precedent. Military officers and men in uniform acquired a new status. They strongly felt that they were indispensable and demanded to play an ever-increasing role in national politics. The military coup d'etat of 1971 marked the manifestation and consolidation of militarism. Amin and his military successors have all shown total distaste for political institutions and establishments. Political parties and allied political forces were outlawed. In effect Uganda has since experienced a facet of militarism from which the population finds it difficult to escape. It is intractable. It has sapped people's energy, caused massive destruction of property and loss of human life on a scale never experienced before. It has been a great hindrance to an all round social and economic development. Because of that, the pace of progress has been slow and the betterment of the quality of life all too little.

After almost forty years of independence, the search for a national political consesus and assurance of a united democratic Uganda continues unabated. The only significant achievememnt to talk of in this sphere is that today we all accept and acknowledge the existance of Uganda as a nation-state.

The formative years of independence witnessed a strong, united, prosperous and peaceful country with a measure of democratic governance and political stability that held out great promise and hope for Uganda. Granted, there were some teething problems. For instance, the country went through the army mutiny of 1964 and was shocked by the events that followed two years later. The political impact of the referendum on the lost counties issue and the eventual political upheaval leading to the 1966 crisis shattered many hopes and forced many people into exile. The upheaval shook almost to breaking-point the nascent and fragile pillars of government and the very existence of national sovereignty and territorial integrity was brought into doubt. Nevertheless, all was not lost.

Drastic measures were taken to save and sustain the nation. To that extent, the significance and experience of the 1966/67 revolution can be equated with:

* The establishment in Britain, in 1689 of the sovereignty of parliament as the central operative principle of Britain's democracy.
* The creation in 1776 of the written American constitution of the Federal Government that is the backbone of the American democratic system
* The assertion of the democratic ideals of liberty and equality of the French Revolution of 1789.

The 1966/67 political developments transformed the National Assembly (Parliament) into a national institution through which all the people of Uganda including representatives from Buganda could and continue up to the present moment to find free expression. Hitherto representatives of Buganda were nominees of the Buganda Lukiko (mini Parliament). They were not directly elected by the population. The revolution also brought to an end any lingering thoughts about secession and created once and for all one political entity called Uganda. It was a realisation of what was foreseen by the 1961 Uganda relationship commission. The commission recommended inter alia: "Secession should be absolutely ruled out and that it seemed impossible to contemplate any other policy that Buganda could reconcile herself to a fruitful relationship". It is gratifying to note that today that fruitful relationship does exist. With a bit of luck and political will, it could be strengthened and improved.

Since then spectacular changes have definitely taken place in terms of population, socio-economic structures and even social attitudes. The society as a whole has been shaken up and recast. But for the most part the intervening sectors have remained largely unaffected with the result that peaceful equilibrium has proved elusive. Thus, the conflicts which characterised the politics of the 1960s have not been effectively addressed. Consequently, the fundamental cleavages of the present are determined in relation to the issues disputed in the past.

For instance, the principle and application of the rule of law have largely been ignored and are yet to take root. The essence of the rule of law is that no person can be punished except for a definite breach of law. The principle also means that all persons are equal before the law. No one should be above ordinary law. Unfortunately, that has not been the case in the Uganda situation of militarism. Throughout the last nearly fifty years, the tendency has been to shift the goal posts when the powers that be deemed it necessary to do so; for example, the lifting of presidential term limits. That state of affairs generates fear among the population and the people are left at the mercy of state agents who are supposed to enforce law and order. The end result is arbitrary arrest or detention and even extra-judicial executions at times.

Laws have often been bent to suit the interests of the regime of the day. During the referendum campaign for the determination of the system of government for Uganda lies were peddled to the effect that the constitution was sacrosanct to the extent that Article 269 of the constitution could not be repealed in order to allow political parties to function normally. But when advocates of mult-partism took their case to court and sought remedy, the Movement government went flat out to amend in record time the very constitution they claimed immutable for purposes of validating the Referendum Provisions Act and a whole range of other measures previously undertaken by the government. That was similar to the 1966 constitution dubbed 'the pigeon-hole constitution'.

The Armed and Security Forces continue to be used to settle political issues. Consider the harassment and intimidation perpetrated by State agents against citizens during the Presidential Elections Campaign of 2006. More often than not, the Commander in Chief has acted outside the provisions of the constitution and the law. Lt. General Yoweri Kaguta Museveni has even had the audacity to invade neighbouring countries with impunity. Just as A.M. Obote failed to adopt dialogue as a method for conflict resolution, the Lt. General was reluctant to hold talks with the armed dissidents who terrorised innocent civilians for years on end.

Ethnicity and religious prejudices are issues that have taken centre stage in the running of government departments and dispensation of services to the people. The question of legitimacy, which haunted the Milton Obote's government after the events of 1966/67, continues to be a source of anxiety for the NRM regime notwithstanding the 1996, 2001, 2006 presidential elections due to the massive rigging experience. While in the 1960s the Kingdoms of Buganda and the Western Region denied legitimacy to the Central Government, advocates of multipartism and the marginalised North were in the forefront in questioning the legitimacy of the regime of the National Resistance Movement.

The form of government is another example of the issues disputed in the past that has not been put to rest. The same subject attracted heated public debate during the Constituency Assembly and for once in many years advocates of multi-partism and the Mengo establishment closed ranks. The NRM had to employ underhanded methods to frustrate the peoples' demand for a federal structure or status for any region that desired it. Indeed, the majority of Districts and Kingdoms continue to clamour for self-determination in terms of controlling and managing local affairs at the local level. The decentralisation scheme put in place by the NRM regime falls far short of the peoples' expectation. If any thing, decentralisation has become a tool for nepotism, patronage, embezzlement of public funds and a conduit of many other mal-practices. It is clear that in the absence of other stimuli, the memory of these issues and other past events can themselves serve as an irritant. Federo was the hottest subject of the debate in Buganda in the campaign for the 2005 referendum."

To confound matters, the major players in the politics of Uganda have been too slow and often reluctant to recognise and accept the personality of the state as opposed to the culture of glorifying the personality of the LEADER (read dictator). The trend of personality-cult continues to blossom despite the proclamation in Article 1 of the 1995 constitution that all political power derives from the people who are sovereign.

Chapter Seventeen

Conclusion

Peace and stability are essential elements for economic development and social progress. It is, therefore, imperative for political leadership at all levels to make every effort to create durable peace and stability.

Therefore, it becomes imperative that everybody must join the crusade for a better future for all that alone justifies the effort and the call for change. Indeed, there are moments in the existence of a nation when people are entitled to ask, "What society do we wish to live in?" And then set out to build the type of community they wish to live in. The constitution making process of 1994/95 could have offered such an opportunity. Unfortunately, the entire electoral process right from the 1988 census to the actual holding of elections whether for the constituency assembly, presidential, parliamentary or local councils was characterised by machinations, fraud and intimidation. Above all, the political playground was not level. Nay, the playground was non-existent. The bulk of Ugandans who believe in building a plural society were denied the right to participate freely. The NRM regime chose to adopt the "mot" attributed to Edgar Pisani "one cock, five hens very good; two cocks, five hens hopeless". The NRM could not read the signs of the times and the High Priest of the Movement felt that his edifice of power was threatened. He remained true to himself in thinking that his concept of politics should be applied to everybody and every organisation. He loathed competitive politics and made sure that there should be no contenders for power in future. Ugandans were subjected to the same scenario in the March 2001 and February 2006 Presidential elections. Such an attitude or situations more often than not breed apathy, rebellion and political instability. The current political leaders and those who aspire to leadership in the future must know that there is an eternal truth about freedom, that is, humanity's desire to control its own destiny. It is within the framework of these freedoms that the people of Uganda can establish the rule of law that provides an environment for stability and development.

Even if the complexities of society and the process by which change comes make it difficult for dictators to contemplate because of their unwillingness and inability to subordinate their personal interests to the common good, there are compelling reasons why the political leadership, including Lt. General Yoweri Kaguta Museveni, must accept change:

* If we do not do so, we shall expose ourselves to factionalism and to a future that will hardly be rosy.
* Uganda would risk falling behind permanently in relation to other African countries and yet with the country's resources, both human and material coupled with the geographical location, Uganda could play a leading role in continental affairs, particularly in the Great Lakes Region.
* the very existence of Uganda as a nation could be threatened once again because of the nature of the fragile society still torn by the ugly old divisions and prejudices.

It would be futile to pretend to determine in advance each of the contours of the envisaged new society the people of Uganda aspire to because that belongs to the future. But it is possible and feasible to sketch out major characteristics of the general liberal society: peace, political stability, the rule of law and access to equal opportunity. With these ingredients in place, the NEW SOCIETY will be in a position to offer new opportunities, recognise talent, foster imagination, respect the dignity of man, acknowledge and admit differences and peculiarities that exist within our diverse cultural heritage. Eventually, that is the society that will transform the daily lives of the ordinary people of this country. Every one of us must adopt the habit of fraternity by replacing scorn, arrogance and indifference with understanding and tolerance. Let every Ugandan reactivate the spirit of national consciousness, which derives from the recognition of the fact that all of us share a common destiny. Uganda needs a fresh start.

Bibliography

Apter, David, E. *The Political Kingdom in Uganda*, Princeton University Press, 1961

Dunbar, A. R. *History of Bunyoro-Kitara*, Oxford University Press, 1965

Dunbar, A. R. *Omukama Chwa 11 Kabalega*, Uganda Famous Men Series, East African Literature Bureau, 1965

Facts about Uganda, Commonwealth Secretariat, Parliamentary Buildings, 1968

Ghali, Boutros Butros, *Unvanquished*, I. B. Tauris Publishers London, New York, 1999

Gukiina, Peter, *Uganda: A Case Study in African Political Development*

Gupta, Vijay, *Obote Second Liberation*, Vikas Publishing House, PVT ltd, 1983

Hancock, Graham, *Lords of Poverty*, Macmillan London Ltd, 1989

Ingham Kenneth, *The Making of Modern Uganda*, London, Allen and Unwin, 1958

Ingham, Kenneth, *History of East Africa,* Longmans, 1962

Ingham, Kenneth, *Politics in Modern Africa: The Uneven Tribal Dimension*, Routledge, London, 1990

Kissinger, Henry, *Years of Renewal*, Simm and Schuster Rockfeller Centre New York,

Kuya, Masette, *Treatise on Political Stability As a Basis for Another Development for Uganda*, Nyon, Switzerland, 1980

Laski, Harold, *Grammar of Politics*, Allen Unwin Ltd 1955

Low and Pratt, *Buganda and British Overrule*

Madison, James, *Federal Papers-Moulding Republic*, The New York Times Co, 1962

Mamdani, Mahmood, *Imperialism and Fascism in Uganda*, Heinemann, Education Books (E.A) Ltd, 1983

May Erskine, *Parliamentary Practice and Procedure*

Mittelman, J. H. *Ideology and Politics in Uganda*, Cornell University Press, New York, 1975

Mudoola, Dan, *Religion, Ethnicity and Politics in Uganda*, Fountain Publishers, Kampala, Uganda, 1993

Mutesa, Sir Edward, *The Desecration of My Kingdom*, London, Constable, 1967

Saro Wiwa, Ken, *A Month and A Day*, A Detention Diary, Penguin Books

Stigliz, Joseph, *Globalization and Its Discontents* Lane, Allen: The Penguin Press, 2002

Thomas and Scott, *Uganda*, Oxford University Press, London 1935

Urquhart, Brian, *Hammarskjold* Alfred Knopf, New York, 1972

Uzoigwe, G. N. *Revolution and Revolt in Bunyoro Kitara*, Makerere History Paper 5, Longman Uganda Ltd, 1970

REPORTS

Investment Programme 1982-84, Uganda Government

Joint Committee on Closer Union in East Africa, Her Majesty's Stationery Office, London

Parliamentary Debates, Hansard, National Assembly/ Council Uganda, 1955-71

Policy Statement: Aims and Objectives, Uganda Asian Action Group, Uganda, 1959

Recovery Programme, Uganda Government Publication, 1981-85

Report of Commission of Inquiry into Gold Allegations, Uganda Government Publication, 1971

Report of the Uganda Relationships Commission Under the Chairmanship of the Rt. Hon.

The Earl of Munster, P. C. K. B. E. Government Printer, Entebbe, 1961

Standing Orders: Uganda National Assembly, *1962-1971*

Select Committees, Procedure and Practice, Her Majesty's Stationery Office Press, 26 November 1958

Uganda: The Case for the Second Republic, Uganda Government Publication, 1971

www.ingramcontent.com/pod-product-compliance
Lightning Source LLC
Chambersburg PA
CBHW030318290526
45785CB00001B/421